Life
AIN'T FOR
Sissies!

Dr. Sugarman's First-Aid Kit
For Your Emotions

Daniel Sugarman, PhD.

Life Ain't for Sissies is based on a series of newspaper columns previously written by Dr. Sugarman's called Psychological First Aid. His columns appeared regularly in Bergen County (N.J.) Newspapers; *The Village Gazette of Ridgewood, The Glen Rock Gazette, The Wyckoff Gazette, The Franklin Lakes Journal, The Ramsey Reporter* and *The Mahwah News*.

ISBN: 978-0-9887703-1-7

First Printing: May 1998
Revised Edition: February 2013
Printed In The United States of America

Contents

✚

Introduction

---·**✛**·---

How would you handle the following situations?

Quiz #1

A) You are on a camping trip and your 8-year-old son spills some boiling water on his leg.

B) Your 17-year-old daughter is slicing some frozen hamburgers. The knife slips and she cuts her palm severely.

C) Dad and you are out at a restaurant celebrating his birthday. Dad is enjoying his steak. As he laughs at your latest joke, a piece of steak lodges in his throat and he begins to choke.

Quiz #2

A) Your 8-year-old son begins to wake up with bad dreams and during the day complains about stomach aches. The doctor finds nothing wrong physically. When you question him, he says, "Mommy, I'm scared all the time."

B) Your 17-year-old daughter becomes increasingly withdrawn and irritable. She loses interest in her friends and becomes preoccupied about her weight.

C) Dad and you are at a restaurant celebrating his birthday. He seems sad. When you question him he says, "Recently life just doesn't seem to be worth living"

Chances are, if you are like most people, you are likely to get better "grades" for your answers to Quiz #1 than for Quiz #2.

As a clinical psychologist with more than 25 years of experience working with adults, children and families, I am astounded that so many people, extremely knowledgeable about first aid for physical complaints, know so little about first aid for psychological problems.

Psychological first aid, like first aid for physical problem, is not designed to replace professional consultation and advice. First aid, whether physical or psychological, can sometimes do the trick if the situation is not severe or persistent.

In this book, I hope to give you some helpful hints in dealing with some of the common problems that we all encounter from time to time.

Research into effective solutions for many of the frequently found psychological difficulties is progressing at an ever increasing rate. Psychologists and other mental heath professionals are finding methods and remedies that can truly help a person to take better charge of their own lives and happiness.

Many of these newer findings are incorporated into these chapters. The case histories are factual, but details are changed and names are disguised in order to maintain my patients' confidentiality.

All of the sections of this book originally appeared as monthly columns in The Gazette newspapers of Bergen County, New Jersey. In each of the columns, I attempted to distill in a readable and concise manner, some of the "First-Aid" measures that a reader might use when dealing with everyday psychological problems.

I have been gratified by the responses I have received from readers who tell me they have found the articles useful and informative. I sincerely hope this book and your own thoughts about the ideas you find here will encourage you to obtain a greater level of insight and gratifying personal growth.

Dr. Daniel Sugarman
Wayne, New Jersey

PART ONE

Life Lesson

CHAPTER 1

Life Ain't for Sissies!
Courage Counts

I remember once, when I was about 5 years old, I fell down and skinned my knee. With the whole family as my audience, I began to make a great fuss. The more they extended their sympathies, the louder were my cries. After the peroxide was applied and the Band-Aid was in place, the assembled crew went back to the task at hand, a large family dinner.

My maternal grandmother, raised in England, gingerly took me aside and said, "Daniel, I know your knee hurts. It's natural to cry when that happens but I think you were making a bit of a fuss. It's terribly important as you grow up to have some *courage!*"

I responded to my grandmother with a typical 5-year-old query. "Why do I need *courage?*" My grandmother, not quite knowing what to reply, thought a moment and then said, "I don't know exactly – I guess it's really not nice to be any other way."

As I grew up, I always remembered my grandmother's words. For a long period of time, I regarded her use of the word *courage* as an outmoded remnant of English Victorian culture.

But as I work more with a variety of patients, many of whom are dealing with difficult situations in their lives, I have become convinced of one thing: Courage counts!

Many of the people I work with in my practice find it hard to acknowledge what they need to do, or have done in the past. Like the cowardly lion in the "Wizard of Oz," some are surprised when I point out to them that they have reserves of courage within them just waiting to be used.

Although I'm a psychologist and not a wizard, I am increasingly impressed with the magic that courage can bring to people who are beset by insecurities and who are assaulted by indecision.

In writing this chapter on courage, I consulted five new basic psychology texts. Curiously, there was no mention, citation or reference in any of these texts of the word *courage*.

Indeed, courage seems an outdated word. But while the word may be outdated, I can assure you that courage is certainly not an outdated concept.

When most of us think of courage, we think of situations such as battlefields, fighting a wild lion or struggling with a car-jacker. Wrongly associated with skydiving and other act of physical bravery, many people make the mistake of relegating courage to heroes. By doing so, they disown the potential for courage that exists within all of us.

Few of us today require the kind of courage that was once needed to guide a Conestoga wagon across a hostile prairie. All of us could use the kind of courage that will guide us through a time in which the old road markers seem to have crumbled. A time in which "anything goes" and any kind of behavior can be rationalized away.

What happened to us? What has happened to the kind of moral fiber that Louis Adamic described as being "a certain blend of courage, integrity, character and principles which has had no satisfactory dictionary name but has been called different things at different time in different countries." Our American name for it is "GUTS."

Let's explore some of the things psychologists do know about courage. First of all, courage tends to be a personal and individual characteristic. What looks courageous to one person might be a "ho –hum" ordinary situation to another. Conversely, what looks to be a simple everyday action for one, could require a great surge of courage for another.

To a casual observer, the professional football player who gets on the field every Sunday afternoon to get knocked around by a bunch of guys with two tons of muscle between them appears to be courageous. To the same casual observer, it might not seem courageous to watch a 14-year-old girl go to the dance floor at the school dance with her 15-year-old boyfriend.

But just as judging a book by its cover can give us wrong answers, judging these two situations without knowing much about the people involved can lead us to the wrong conclusion.

For the football player, playing a Sunday afternoon game may be a part of a rather boring "so-what" routine that may in no way be a challenge to muster up courage. For the 14-year-old girl, in the midst of adolescent turmoil, getting up on the dance floor in front of her classmates, when every nerve and bone in her body would like to flee, may require a tremendous amount of bravery. Who, indeed, is more courageous? The football player or the 14-year-old adolescent?

To be afraid is human and many people confuse courage with not being afraid. In reality, true courage occurs when we *move through* our fears and do what we need to do even though our knees are knocking together. The late Admiral "Bull" Halsey once commented about heroes. He said, "There are no great men – only great challenges that ordinary men are forced by circumstances to meet!"

So courage is not the same as not being afraid. All sensitive people will do whatever they can to avoid unnecessary pain. But when our backs are up against a wall, we sometimes tap into our own resources of courage.

Almost all of you know some people who have demonstrated great courage in their lives when the chips are down. Psychologists know that some people act courageously in their lives because they where lucky when growing up to have parents who modeled courageous attitudes. One woman I know went through horrible experiences during World War II. Living in Europe in a city that was continuously being bombed, her house was bombed and destroyed within a few months. Shortly after this, her father was killed in an air raid. As if these tragedies were not enough, a younger sister died of disease.

Growing up amidst these disasters seemed almost impossible, if it hadn't been for the attitude of her mother who steadfastly resolved and taught her children, by word and deed, to move through terrible times.

Now a mature women, this child of a brave mother has absorbed her mother's teachings and recently has been able to handle many different situations in a courageous manner. By doing so, she has eased the pain and suffering for herself as well as her family.

The English author, Thomas Carlyle once wrote, "Every man has a coward and a hero in his soul." Which would you rather be?

If you decide to move in the direction of greater courage, which, in the long run, will make things easier for everyone including yourself, here are some tips that can help the cowardly lion that lurks inside to find his way to the Emerald Castle at the end of the Yellow Brick Road.

1) Have the Courage to Exercise Your Power of Choice

The capacity to shape our lives is a pain and privilege. The great French philosopher and writer Jean Paul Sartre once wrote, "I *am* my choices."

Recent psychological research has shown that, contrary to outdated notions, we always have *some* choice in the problems that life hands to us for solution.

When the famous Austrian psychiatrist, Dr. Victor Frankel, was a young physician, he was interned in a Nazi concentration camp. There he observed unspeakable acts of torture, mass murders, and brutality – the likes of which defies description.

Dr. Frankel observed those inmates who survived and those who rapidly succumbed. He noted the survivors tended to be the people who chose to affirm life even in the living hell of the concentration camp. Some of these survivors chose to help others even less fortunate than themselves by administering to their physical needs. Others chose to comfort others by pointing out the beauty of a sunset or the taste of rainwater on a parched tongue. These inmates had *no* choice whether or not they would live or die. They did have some choice *what they would do* while they were awaiting almost certain death.

Miraculously surviving these hellish conditions, Dr. Frankel returned to practice as a psychiatrist in Vienna. As a result of his concentration camp experiences, he became convinced that *choice* was a key element in helping people retain or regain emotional health. His theories and methods centered on the power of choice have been adopted by many therapists across the world.

In my own practice, I observe how patients begin to improve once they make the decision to have the courage to exercise their power of choice.

A year or so ago, for example, I saw a couple for some marital counseling. They had been married for eight years and had two children. Their marriage was marked by almost constant conflict, brief separations and some previous attempts to receive some counseling. When I saw the husband alone for a few sessions, it was clear that he was confused as to what he wanted to do with his marriage. As I listened to him carefully, I realized he had always been ambivalent about being married and remaining faithful to one woman. Even on his honeymoon he had feelings such as, "now I'll never be able to be with another women again." Years later, still obsessing about whether or not he should get a divorce, he asked my advice as to what he should do. I told him that he would have to make up his own mind but my suggestion to him was that he should probably *get married* before he got a divorce!! As we continued to speak, he began to realize that a large part of the problems he was having arose from the fact that he never completely committed himself to the decision that he made years ago – to marry. With one foot in and the other foot out it was no wonder there were so many hectic and horrible times. When he did commit to the relationship, there was considerable improvement and more happiness than there had been for a long time.

2) When Necessary – Have the Courage to Go Against the Crowd

It is not easy to go against the crowd – even when the silent, faint voice of our conscious tells us that we are right. We are all enormously influenced by others and sometimes it takes a lot of guts to stand up to a crowd or a person in authority.

In one classic experiment, Yale College students were asked to participate in a psychological study in which students were told they were to investigate the effect of punishment on learning. As part of the experiment, the students were asked to administer a small electric shock to the subjects (in fact, the subjects were con-federates of the experiment and did not receive any shocks at all).

As the experiment progressed, the student was urged by the professor to increase the level of shock. The subjects, confederates of the professor, acted as if they were in great pain. Sad to relate, the great majority of these bright, well-educated Yale students complied with the professors urging to increase the level of the shock even though they observed that these actions were causing great pain. Only a small minority of the students refused to go along with the professor's instructions and had the courage to stand up for something they believed to be right.

It is not easy to ride the displeasure of a crowd or of an authority figure and it takes real courage to do so. As a child, how many times did you stand by while a weaker classmate was being assaulted or taunted by the class bully? Even though you knew it was wrong? As an adult, how many times have you remained quiet when a group you were with might be uttering ugly racial comments? How often have you listened to malicious gossip about someone else without defending the victim?

Do you want to feel better about yourself? Try to have the courage to do the right thing, even though it might be displeasing to those around you. By maintaining your own unique blend of integrity and principle, you can get in touch with your own inner vitality and, in just the way the muscles in your body become stronger if you swim upstream, your emotional resources will develop if you are willing to resist a popular opinion or harmful action that simply isn't right for you.

3) Have the Courage to Think Long Term

So often, when we are confronted with a choice of a decision, we have to choose between immediate gratification and long-term pleasure.

When we make our decisions in favor of a future possibility, rather than a selfish immediate gain, we are able to feel pride in our choice and are strengthened.

All around us, we are bombarded with appeals to the baby within us – rather than the adult. The baby wants immediate gratification with little thought for long-term payment or pleasure. The adult within us knows that there is really No Free Lunch and that eventually a debt that is incurred must be paid in the future. During the past few years I have seen many people who, by giving in to immediate pleasure, find long-term trouble. In the course of a year, they took several expensive trips, none of which they could really afford, through the apparent magic of charging with plastic. They amassed debts on several credit cards that eventually resulted in personal bankruptcy.

To some extent the age-old story of Faust, who sold his soul to the devil for a few brief moments of happiness, is truly a parable for modern-day Americans. In our quest for immediate happiness, we so often find long-term pain.

If we are wise, we try to focus, not so much on our immediate but on our long-term happiness.

One patient of mine, now a recovered alcoholic, spent years of his life in and out of all kinds of problems caused by his drinking. He had been in rehabilitation and AA many times, until he finally managed about five years ago to cease drinking. When I asked him when he felt was the crucial factor in allowing his recovery, he thought awhile and said, "when I wanted a drink, I knew I would enjoy it, but then I projected myself into the next day and remembered how I would have that awful feeling of nausea and nervousness and fatigue. By thinking of the future I can control the now."

Are you on a diet? Want that piece of cake? Sure you do! Think about how you will feel in a bathing suit next summer. It is not easy to say "NO" to the baby that exists within all of us. But when we do, we can take pride in the courage that we have shown in choosing life and growth and future happiness rather than immediate gratification!

4) Have the Courage to Rejoice in What You Have

All too many people lose their courage when they begin to dwell on what they *lack* rather than what they *have*. Life, like a tangled reel of motion picture film, consist of a series of "moments" that are spliced together. If we can teach ourselves to evaluate our assets on each "frame" we can influence the final ending. Each stage of our lives brings satisfaction with it; the power to bring joy to *all* of the stages of our lives is a measure of our *courage*.

To some extent, psychologists know that the amount of unhappiness we have in our lives is in direct proportion to the degree of discrepancy between where we are and where we would like to be. In American culture we are bombarded by consumer oriented advertising that urges us to do more, buy more, have more. The next thing we need should be bigger, newer, better, etc. Infantile "wants" often become elevated to the level of needs.

Never before in the history of the country have so many Americans had so much. Telephones, televisions, automobiles, homes – and all of those material items that were once regarded as luxuries for the wealthy are now commonplace items available to the great majority of our citizens. Supermarkets are stocked with food all year round. The world economy and modern technology make it possible to have raspberries in winter and frozen food in the summer.

Our homes can be made warm when it is cold and cool when it is hot. Few people have to put on an overcoat and trudge through the snow if they need to go to the bathroom on a cold winter night.

Just one hundred years ago in America, and right now in much of the world, the comforts that we have would be regarded as luxuries only available to royalty or in fantasy!

In spite of this wonderful reality, I see so many people who are so unhappy because they can't quite finance a brand-new sport vehicle or can't afford to add the extra playroom to the house. When people concentrate on what they don't have, rather than what assets they do possess, they lose their sense of "spunk" and often spend many unhappy hours wasting time on the "self pity potty."

When you become brave enough to rejoice in what you have rather than torturing yourself with what you don't have, a sense of courageous joy can return.

5) Life Ain't for Sissies!

If you can't take bad news, you had better stop reading now. The bad news, the news that most people know but do their best to forget, is that *life is tough!* Yes! It is rough and tough and it is worse for those faint of heart.

From the moment of birth, struggle is an essential feature of life. Have you ever watched a baby learning to walk? They stand only to fall. They stand again and fall and bruise their nose. They cry, are comforted and try again. Finally, they learn to walk.

Can you remember the struggle that you had when you tried to learn to read? What were all those squiggly lines? Why can Mike and Susie figure it out so fast and I don't get it? Do you remember all the pain you had when you fell off your bike and scraped your knees? The terrible night when you had a stomach virus and thought you could never again look at another hamburger? Can you recall how scary it was leaving your parents and going to camp or college for the first time?

Can you still feel the sting of rejection when the person you loved best in high school went out with someone else? The anxiety of finding a job and disappointment of not getting a promotion? How about the pain of having to take care of your elderly parents only to have them die?

Yes! From womb to tomb, life gives us a series of challenges.

There are disappointments, losses, broken hopes, and shattered dreams. Our popular culture does much to shield us from the reality that life contains struggle. In many ways our ancestors, who expected life to be tough, had an easier time dealing with struggle. The struggle and challenges of life were accepted and expected. Today, all too many of us feel we are somehow one of the worlds "losers" if we have to cope with the *inevitable* challenges and struggles that the excitement of life brings to us all. When we bravely confront the sea of troubles that await us with an attitude of optimism, hope and pride in ourselves for dealing directly with the struggle, a curious thing occurs: the struggles, disappointments, and troubles somehow become more manageable.

We work our way out of the storm and into the sun again. Today, perhaps more then ever before, COURAGE COUNTS!!

PART TWO

Common Conditions

CHAPTER 2

Battling Boredom

"Against boredom even the gods themselves struggle in vain!"
~ NIETZSCHE

"The two foes of human happiness are pain and boredom."
~ SCHOPENHAUER

Nietzsche, Schopenhauer and many other astute observers of the human condition throughout the centuries have all recognized the tremendous toll that boredom can exact, not only on our happiness, but on our health as well. Recent studies have shown that prolonged boredom can change aspects of our body chemistry that could eventually compromise our state of health and well-being.

While boredom has always seemed to be part of the human condition, both the incidence and complaints about boredom seem to be on the increase. What's it all about?

Psychologists know that boredom can arise from many different causes. First and foremost, we become bored if we do not receive a changing amount of external stimulation. A marked reduction of visual, auditory, or tactile stimulation can severely disrupt our very functioning. In one experiment designed to learn about the effects of boredom on astronauts, students were placed in a situation of total sensory deprivation. Their vision and hearing were blocked and even tactile stimulation was removed. After a brief period of time, these subjects became grossly uncomfortable. Many began to hallucinate and show other signs of severe mental disturbances that did not abate until they began to receive more sensory stimulation.

Another cause of boredom can come from feelings that are bottled up and not expressed. If we find ourselves in a situation where we are angry, for example, but we cannot for one reason or another express that anger, we often begin to feel a state of vague fatigue, lack of interest, and boredom.

A gnawing, even painful, sense of boredom will often arise in a situation where we are not challenged and where we are unable to use our fullest talents. Psychologists know that in order to feel well and alive, we need a certain amount of challenge and the opportunity to use our potential.

For example, during the Great Depression of the 1930s, millions of Americans were out of work. Each advertised job would bring thousands of hopeful applicants. One well-known department store decided to fill all of its positions as elevator operators and porters with only college graduates. After a brief period on the job many of these newly hired professionals got bored, ill and would miss work. Many of them insulted customers and had fights with their fellow employees. Investigating this unhappy situation revealed that the underlying culprit for the poor job performance was painful chronic boredom. These college graduates were under-challenged and frustrated in their inability to use their potential and talents.

Another common cause of boredom is related to living out someone else's script and not finding meaning in one's own life. One patient of mine, for example, was recently retired. Many of his close friends were avid golfers and for the first year or so he played golf almost every day. After a while, he felt that he had had enough but at the urging of his friend, he continued to remain part of their foursome. Not following his own script resulted in a vague sense of depression and chronic boredom. Finally he had the courage to resist the friendly pressure that was place on him by his golf buddies and he became a volunteer in a literacy program. Now, happily involved in an activity that gives him a sense of meaning, he is back to enjoying golf again – but only once or twice a week.

Only a very lucky few escape boredom. Most of us, however, need to battle at least occasional bouts of boredom. In our own battle with boredom here are some *psychological first-aid tips*:

1) What do I Really Want?

Many periods of boredom arise when we no longer listen to our own inner voice and when we refuse to listen to our inner needs. One young lawyer that I knew had a lucrative, prestigious position with a New York law firm. After several years of practicing corporate law, she became increasingly bored and restless. Although it meant a marked cut in salary, she finally found the inner strength to move into an area of law that held great challenge for her and now she works as an assistant public prosecutor.

Almost without realizing it, most of us get caught up with the routine of everyday life. We begin to conform to subtle and sometimes not-so-subtle social pressures and the many "shoulds" and "should nots" of others. As this occurs, we may often lose touch with our own inner needs. When you are bored, a good way of beginning your search for greater satisfaction and happiness is to ask yourself, "what do *I* really want?"

2) Drive Home a New Way

Whether we realize it or not, most of us get caught up in routines of sameness. We wake up at 6:45 am and take a shower.

We have Corn Flakes for breakfast and catch the 8:05 train to work. After work, we watch Monday Night Football or go bowling on Tuesday nights. Before we go to bed, we brush our teeth and read a chapter of a mystery. On Sunday afternoons, we visit Mom and Dad and at the end of July, we spend two weeks at the shore. Little wonder we get bored!!

Like an old blanket, a strict routine can bring us a sense of comfort and belonging, but like a blanket that can get too heavy, we can become suffocated. When you find that you are bored, start experimenting with your usual routines in little ways. Try having an English muffin for breakfast rather than cereal. Spend a night watching a special on public television rather than your usual program. Think about going to a lake in Maine rather than the shore next summer. Consciously taking steps to be adventuresome and to find alternative routes will allow you to drive home in a new and hopefully satisfying way.

3) Make Something

Buying a fresh loaf of bread in a bakery or a wonderful prepared meal in a gourmet supermarket are conveniences that your grand parents could never have dreamed of. But like most things in life, there is No Free Lunch. By buying bread or a pre-made meal, we *gain* a lot of convenience and time, but we *lose* the pleasure and activity of kneading the dough and the smell of the bread baking or the chicken roasting.

Since so much of the boredom of modern life arises from our loss of creativity of doing everyday chores, a quick fix for boredom often involves making something. Knitting an afghan, assembling a birdhouse or cooking a new recipe provides us with the sense of gratification that can dispel a boggy bout of boredom.

4) Learn Something

Evidence suggests that boredom arises when we are not using our full potential. Imagine, if you will, how rusty and dull a Super-16 cylinder sports car would become if it was never allowed to drive more than 25 mph! In my work with people, I know that many folks never use their full mental, emotional or physical horsepower. While we have been built and endowed with the potential for high performance functioning in many areas, we often limp along on five or eight or ten of our 16 cylinders. When we live in this kind of condition for a long time, like a car, we become rusty and dull. In some ways, however, we feel something that a car is incapable of feeling: a state of chronic, insidious, energy-stealing boredom!

The lubricant that can get us moving smoothly again is often learning a new skill or revisiting an old interest. Along with the problems that arise from living in a congested suburban area close to a major city, we also have many blessings. We are, indeed, lucky to have all kinds of opportunities to broaden our horizons and to learn new skills. In this area, there are numerous well-run adult schools that offer literally hundreds of courses. Just for the asking and an investment in time and money, we can learn to build some shelves, cook a Japanese meal, or speak French. If we choose, we can attend one of our excellent community colleges and learn skills that could help us use a computer or start an investment program. So many of us would kick away the "Boredom Blues" if we could just allow ourselves the joy and challenge of learning something new.

5) Ask Yourself "Why am I here?"

Boredom often sets in when we lose a sense of meaning and purpose. The existential philosophers have pointed out to us that we human beings – and only human beings – share a scary piece of knowledge. We, in contrast to all the other living creatures who share this troubled planet with us, know something very strange. We know that we are here for only a limited amount of time. Used improperly, this sense of our own eventual mortality can make us feel sad and hopeless. Used properly however, this knowledge can make us realize that we almost always have some degree of choice. We can choose to make the world a better place or we can sink into maudlin self-absorption.

One way or another, you need to find a sense of purpose and meaning in your life. Some may choose to explore the sense of meaning that organized religion offers, while others may choose to find a sense of purpose in more secular activities. One person I know finds purpose and meaning in caring for his two grandchildren while another finds gratification in bringing pets into a nursing home and watching the joy that this simple act bring. Still another teaches Sunday school and takes pride in watching the children learn and grow.

What SOUNDS right, or would FEEL right, for you?

CHAPTER 3

Dealing with Depression:
The Common Cold of Emotional Disorders

Like a dark cloud that obscures the sun, depression can cover over our feelings of joy and happiness. Just the way the appearance of a cloud can be brief and fleeting or dense and long-lasting, feelings of depression can range from a fleeting day or two of the "blues" or the "blahs" to months or even years of incapacitating unhappiness.

While everyone feels depression in their own unique way, there are certain symptoms that are almost always present. Restlessness, loss of concentration, insomnia, change in eating patterns, unexplained fatigue, vague aches and pains, instability, and, above all, a sense of sadness and hopelessness should make us suspect that depression is the culprit.

It is normal to experience some depression following a loss or after a severe blow to our self-esteem. However, sometimes this temporary normal state of sadness deepens and begins to affect our happiness and functioning. It is during these times that it is important to take steps to cut depression down to its proper size.

Depression is so frequent that it is often referred to as the common cold of emotional disorders. It has no respect for class, race, age or sex. Paupers and princes alike have endured the suffering that depression can bring. Abraham Lincoln, Queen Victoria, William Styron and Buzz Aldrin are among the millions of others around the world who have experienced painful bouts of depression. It has been reliably estimated that at any *one* time approximately 14 million Americans are seriously depressed and a far greater number of people experience a milder form of depression.

Because depression is so prevalent and so emotionally and financially draining, scientists from many disciplines are rapidly zeroing in on its causes and cures; so there are many current theories and treatments available.

Some psychologists and psychiatrists feel that serious depression sets in after a long period of unresolved stress. In some manner, our stress reserves become exhausted. Depression, therefore, can be seen as a form of "depletion." When this occurs, certain biochemical changes may occur in our brain and this temporary chemical imbalance can cause a myriad of depressive symptoms. Some people, because of their genetic make-up, are more susceptible to depression than others who might be biologically programmed to respond to stress in a different fashion.

Other psychologists and psychiatrists feel that the source of depression can be found in angry feelings that are not expressed and are then turned "inward." Still other scientists are convinced that depression is the result of patterns of faulty thinking in which a person consistently views the world through "black-tinted" glasses and sees every situation as the beginning of a negative event.

Recently, many psychologists have convincing evidence that depression often results from a state of so-called "learned helplessness." When a person feels there is nothing they can do, they simply "give up" and when they stop resisting, they sink rapidly into a state of depression.

From my own clinical work experience with many patients, I am convinced that all these theories are really pieces of the same jigsaw puzzle of depression.

The good news is that with competent treatment almost everyone who is depressed can be helped. The bad news is that many people still view depression as some sort of character flaw or as a sign of weakness.

If your depression is severe or long-lasting, you should certainly consider professional help. With or without professional help, here are several psychological "first-aid" tips that can help you lift the clouds of depression.

1) Spot Check Your Thinking

Many research studies indicate that many depressed people constantly make errors in their thinking. They have learned to see everything around them as being a result of their faults or lack of ability. They often indulge in a form of erroneous thinking called "over-generalization." For example, one depressed patient of mine was an extremely gifted legal stenographer. Her employers valued her work and her accuracy. One day, in a marathon rush to type a legal brief, she made two typographical errors which her employer asked her to correct. She appeared at my office the next day depressed and tearful. When asked what was troubling her, she told me that she was "a failure" as a stenographer. When she was able to correct her *thinking* so that it was more realistic, she accepted the fact that *everyone* makes an error or two. *Are you thinking realistically about events in your life?*

2) Get Comfortable with Your Anger

Anger is a part of life and a natural reaction to frustration. Handling anger properly is a great skill. *Exploding* with anger rarely helps. "Stuffing" anger often can result in *implosion* that may cause depression. In dealing with depression your goal is to identify the source of your anger and to learn not to feel guilty about your feelings. You are responsible not for what you *feel* but for what you *do* with your feelings. You must learn to express your anger in an appropriate manner that can help undo the source of your frustrations.

3) Take Care of Your Body

The ancient Greeks knew that it was impossible to have a "sound mind" unless you also had a "sound body."

Too often in our rush for miracle drugs and quick fixes, we forget this *ancient wisdom*. Many people who are depressed can improve their mental outlook by simply taking better care of their bodies. Lack of rest and sleep can result in a sense of fatigue which often deepens into depression. Not exercising our bodies makes us feel sluggish and dull. Alcohol, which is often used by people to lift spirits, plays a cruel trick by actually producing a state of depression. Indeed, depression and alcoholism are twin sisters of despair. Often, when heavy drinkers stop drinking, they are surprised by how much their mood improves after a period of several weeks.

4) Are You Getting a Payoff From Your Depression?

Sometimes, a person who is depressed has learned (often unconsciously) that being the unhappy victim and staying sad has its special rewards.

One college student I knew learned that each time she would begin to cry to her boyfriend about her dorm conditions and her roommate, he would try to cheer her up by taking her to a movie or to dinner. Without realizing it, rewarding her behavior in this manner, only served to increase her depressive behavior. After awhile, the boyfriend became disgusted with her constant unhappiness and found himself another girlfriend who had a more balanced view of life.

When someone is sad or complains, most friends and close associates are initially sympathetic. After awhile, however, people withdraw their support and the depressed person is more lonely then ever. Is anyone you know "rewarding" your sad mood by giving you some special privilege or attention? Think hard!

Do! Do! Do!

Recent research points to the fact that both people and animals can learn to be helpless.

In one classic experiment dogs in a laboratory learned they could not escape a harmless but slightly painful electric shock. When these dogs were later placed in a situation where they could, in fact, escape the shock, they did nothing. They had *learned to be helpless.*

Many people, after a series of frustrating failures or disappointments, simply give up and give in. Like the dogs in the laboratory, they have learned to be hopeless and they generalize their helplessness and pessimism to new situations which, in reality, they could do something about. In the last analysis, *depression is a disease of hope.*

When you are sad or down, your greatest enemy is inactivity and passivity. To combat this tendency, it is important to stay active and involved. If one solution does not seem to work, try another. If a second doesn't work, try a third. Start becoming involved in new and constructive activities. Learn a new skill, play some tennis, volunteer at a shelter for the homeless. Return to some of the healthy activities that used to bring you pleasure.

If, after a period of self-help you find you are still depressed, do yourself a favor and get the help of a qualified professional person who can be your ally in your battle against the blues.

YOU CAN WIN!!

CHAPTER 4

Facing Your Anxiety:
The Sweaty Palm Syndrome

P sychological first-aid, like first-aid for physical problems, is not designed to replace professional consultation and advice. However, first-aid, whether physical or psychological, can sometimes do the trick if the situation is not severe or persistent. Psychologists know that we all experience anxiety from time to time. It is estimated that at least 25 million Americans suffer from anxiety conditions and many more experience the pangs of anxiety to a lesser degree. Sweaty palms, insomnia, fatigue, shortness of breath, and a constant state of worry are all clues that anxiety is lurking about.

When confronted with stress, our bodies prepare for the "fight or flight" response – a natural physiological reaction. With this, our blood pressure rises, adrenaline sends messages to our brain to release fuel for our muscles and our pupils begin to dilate.

These reactions were helpful to our acceptors who needed to fight tigers or flee from mastodons. However, for modern man, most of the stresses of life have nothing to do with tigers or mastodons. They have more to do with paying our mortgage, dealing with a rebellious adolescent, or finding a good nursing home for our aging parents. Nevertheless, our bodies still react physically, in the same manner as ancient man. As a result of this physiological occurrence, we begin to stew in our own stress hormones.

While some anxiety is inevitable – and, indeed, a healthy and necessary part of living – the feeling of anxiety is almost always unpleasant. Although we can never rid ourselves of anxiety, psychologists know that there are many "First-Aid" measures we can take to reduce some of the aches of anxiety. Here are some tips I've found to be helpful to my patients when they are confronting a bout of anxiety.

1) Treat Yourself to a Good Physical Examination

Often, when people experience anxiety, there is excessive worry about health. For example, each headache is imagined to be the beginning of a brain tumor. Every muscle twitch is feared to be the herald of a rare and exotic neurological disease. Every stomach ache is perceived to be the start of an illness that's bound to be terminal.

A good and thorough physical exam can often calm such fears as being groundless, which then helps both doctor and patient label the symptoms by their right name: Anxiety.

In a few cases, some physical conditions – hyperthyroidism, for example, which produces symptoms similar to anxiety – can be diagnosed and treated.

2) Don't be Bluffed by Anxiety

One well-known psychiatrist tells her patients, "anxiety is distressing but it is not dangerous."

Indeed, one of the most helpful things to keep in mind during a bout of anxiety is that, while the symptoms are unpleasant, they will pass. It is important to realize that most anxiety is temporary. If we accept a period of anxiety as a normal response to a stressful period in our lives, we get through the unpleasantness much more quickly. *Fear of fear* is our worst enemy.

3) Cool the Self-Demands

Most people who experience excessive anxiety are perfectionist – they make excessive demands on themselves. They feel the need to always be in control and they have learned to worry about not living up to some imaginary standards.

For many people, a state of anxiety can be reduced by giving up the dream of being Superman or Wonder Woman. We are all human and we all make mistakes. While we can try to improve, we need to be patient and forgiving to ourselves, just as a loving parent would teach a child.

4) Watch What You are Telling Yourself

Most anxiety sufferers have learned to think in a somewhat distorted manner. They often elevate possibilities into probabilities. If you are going to drive into the city, it is indeed possible that your car can be hit by a truck. The probability of this occurring is very low. If your daughter complains of a soar throat, it is certainly possible that this could be the first stages of leukemia. The probability is that she is getting a common cold.

When you train yourself to think more in terms of probabilities rather than possibilities, you will find your "worry machine" will stop being so overwhelmed.

5) Exercise Helps a Lot!

Many of our symptoms of anxiety can be almost diminished or eliminated through the use of exercise.

As our natural response to anxiety and stress is to "fight or flee," when we exercise we literally "fool" our bodies by a brisk walk, a jog, jazzercise class, or a long bike ride, etc.

Exercise, particularly of the aerobic and vigorous variety, releases hormones that produce a sense of well-being and safety. Regular exercise promotes better sleep, better appetite, and can raise our energy levels. For example, a recent study compared the effects of exercise on a group of navy personnel at sea. Those sailors assigned to an exercise group reported much less stress then their shipmates who did not exercise.

6) Talk It Out

Almost all of us have had the experience of having our anxieties attenuated and relieved after we shared our feelings.

Our language is filled with expressions that indicate the helpful effect that verbalizing our worries can have. Common expressions such as "I'm glad I got it off my chest" or "I feel much better since I got it out" are part of that.

Putting our anxieties and fears into words helps us sort out our feelings. Often, in talking about our problems, we cut them down to a manageable size or see solutions that previously eluded us. Rather than doing this, many anxious people sit and brood; in doing so magnify their fears and worries.

One thing, though, is that when we decide to talk about our anxieties and worries, we need to exercise good judgment regarding the person we are going to talk with. A good confidant is someone who will listen and understand. He/she will *not* give unsolicited advice, nor tell you that "you should do this or that."

Above all, he/she will guard your confidentially and privacy.

If you are not sure that anyone you know fits this profile, or if you want some professional assistance, it might be time to have a consultation with a trained professional.

With a little patience, time and assistance almost everyone can find some relief from painful feelings of anxiety.

CHAPTER 5

That Strange Friend Called Anger

Perhaps of all the emotions, people have the most difficulty handling anger.

Psychologists know that anger is a necessity, albeit sometimes unpleasant feeling. How we handle our anger can make an enormous difference in our interpersonal relationships, our health and our very civilization. Fire, if correctly used can warm our homes and fuel engines but, if allowed to get out of control, can burn down our homes and consume us. Anger if harnessed, can be a powerful force for positive action; anger, out of control, can spark conflagrations of destruction.

Our propensity for anger exists deep within the structure of our brain and is part of our evolutionary heritage. When we are confronted with frustration, this "anger center" in our brain becomes alerted and our bodies become mobilized to do something about the frustrating situation. Take a favorite toy away from a baby or prevent a first grader from watching his favorite TV program and you will see anger in its natural state.

When our ancient ancestors lived in caves, dealing with anger was, in many ways, much simpler. If someone took something from you that was valued, you would hit them on the head with your club. They, in turn, would hit you back and eventually someone would come out the winner (if, in fact, they survived the fight).

In our slow and painful march out of these primitive emotional swamps towards a degree of civilization, the handling of anger has become much more complicated. We, who were taught not to hit each other, sometimes mix up the message. Sometimes, in addition to learning not to solve problems by hitting, we come to believe that anger *itself* is wrong.

In my practice as a clinical psychologist, I see many people on a daily basis who struggle with anger. Handled poorly, anger can be grossly destructive to oneself or to others. We now know that explosive expression of angry feelings only serves to make the situation worse and further feed the river of rage. An explosion of anger in the form of screaming, yelling, and letting it "all hang out" may bring some very temporary relief, but more often, long-term problems result.

As destructive as an "explosion" of anger can be, an "implosion," in which anger is turned against ourselves or is completely denied, can be even more dangerous.

Recent research has demonstrated that how we handle our anger can have marked and direct effects upon our health and a whole variety of medical conditions seem to be related partially to the way in which we deal with our hostility.

Researchers at Duke University, for example, have now demonstrated that hostility is a risk factor for coronary artery disease and plays a role that is perhaps as important as elevated cholesterol and diet.

These scientists have found that chronically irritable people – you know the kind – put themselves at greater risk of heart disease. Example: not being able to tolerate an older driver who is moving slowly on the road, they lean on the horn; not being willing to wait in a supermarket line when the person in front of them fumbles with her purse, they make some snide or sarcastic remarks. By doing so, they are unwittingly doing some serious damage to their own coronary arteries. Other techniques for dealing with anger can be equally ineffective and, indeed, sometimes destructive!

Some people express their anger by shutting down and withdrawing from others. One poet wrote that we can kill with fire or we can kill with ice. The "shut-downers" manage to hurt those around them by coating everyone with a thick layer of frosty indifference. One woman, for example, when angry at her teenage daughter and then at her husband for being too lenient with her, would "shut down" for days at a time. As a result, the issue never got fully discussed nor did they ever get resolved.

A variation of "shutting down" is sulking. When a person uses sulking as a way of expressing anger, they clearly broadcast the message to all around them that they are unhappy, and in a variety of ways, manage to spoil the fun of all those who are near them. Sulking is, in the last analysis, and adult version of the old-fashioned childish temper-tantrum.

Others, when angry, never deal with the person they are angry with. They displace the anger on those who are more defenseless and make easy targets. Several years ago, there was a cartoon that beautifully illustrated this mechanism of displacement. In the first box, there is a picture of a boss chewing out his vice president. The second box showed the vice president coming home and yelling at his wife. In the third, the wife yells at the child, and in the fourth, the child kicks the cat out the door. As the cat is flying through the air, there is a quizzical expression on his face – *What happened?*

Still others deal with their anger by becoming extremely competitive with everyone and anyone. A driver passing the person on the road is seen as a direct insult. One patient of mine, an extremely angry, competitive, successful business executive, while going to see a ball game, started to walk down the aisle towards his seat. Another man, also going for his seat somehow walked in front of him. My patient, viewing this as a major issue, insulted the other man and a fight broke out. Forty stitches and one broken jaw later, my patient commented "I think I have to find better ways to deal with my anger." Indeed!!

1) Learn to Spot the Feelings

Identifying anger in yourself is not as easy as it would seem. Because many of us have been trained not to be angry. Anger can wear many disguises: Gossip, physical symptoms, depression and forgetting something that is important to someone else are some of the common costumes that masks underlying hostility. Anger is usually most difficult to identify if it arises from the frustration caused by someone we truly love. One woman, for example, found that there were times in her relationship with her fiancé where, and seemingly without warning, she would experience feelings of anxiety and increased muscular tension. She would also become aware of a mild headache and a feeling that she was about to cry. After some serious introspection, she came to realize that these feelings would arise after her fiancé would disappoint or frustrate her in some way. He might, for example, arrive at her home late or would cancel a date made previously. It took her some time to realize she was, in fact, angry. Because she was a rather insecure person, she was afraid, that any expression of anger towards her fiancé might jeopardize the relationship. In reality, the only thing that was jeopardized was her own heath and happiness. When she learned to handle her anger in an effective manner, she not only felt better but, in fact, the relationship with her fiancé got better as well.

2) Load Your Brain Before You Shoot Your Mouth

An ancient proverb tell us that "Anger is the wind that blows out the lamp of the mind."

Modern psychologists have confirmed the validity and wisdom of this proverb. When we are in a rage, we are under the influence of our primitive "animal" brain. The more advanced, civilized part of our brain – indeed, the very parts that make us fully human – are out of commission. When we are in a white-hot rage, we are likely to do things and say things which we will later come to regret. Sometimes, there will be no turning back from the things we say or do at such times.

One man I knew was furious at his wife. In a child-like rage, he got into his car and backed out of his driveway. In his effort to speed away, he neglected to see that his three-year-old daughter was on her tricycle. After three months in a coma, she died. This man, 10 years later, is still haunted by the memory of that disastrous and tragic day.

I'm sure that if you honestly examine your own life, you will find some areas of regret and shame because of deeds or words that emerged during a period of anger. It's important to remember there are very few provoking situations that require an immediate response or reply. When you feel your blood begin to boil, it's time to get out of the oven and cool yourself down a bit. If you don't, you may, in fact, boil over and scald everyone in sight – even yourself!

Some people feel that taking a 20 minute time-out period is helpful; others use an "I'll sleep on it" recipe. Still others might employ the time-honored "count to 10" routine.

It's not important which of these techniques you use as long as you "load your brain before you shoot your mouth!"

3) Talk It Out

Talking about our feelings can be the lubricant that smooths out our lives. By talking, we not only release feelings in an appropriate, harmless manner, but we often can arrive at solutions that can help us repair a problem or a damaged relationship.

One young lawyer I knew, for example, worked for a large firm. In spite of his excellent work, he found that he was never promoted. Every few months he was in the frustrating situation of seeing his colleagues getting promoted or receiving raises. One day, after a much more junior colleague was promoted, he was in a rage. He called me on the phone and told me that he was going to quit that afternoon and he was about to tell his boss once and for all what he could do with his job.

I urged him to "sleep on it" for a couple days. After he cooled down a bit, he decided that it would make more sense for him to talk to his boss calmly about his disappointment and his feelings about being "passed up." He made an appointment and he expressed his feelings in a measured, mature manner. During this conversation, his boss listened intently and told him that, while everyone regarded his work as excellent, the reason that he wasn't being promoted was related to the fact that many of the secretaries in the firm felt that he was overly demanding and abrupt.

After a cordial discussion that lasted more than two hours, both men understood each other's position. After the conversation, the young lawyer realized that his boss had made some sense and he was able to become much more cordial and understanding in dealing with office personnel. A year later, he was promoted and got his raise.

When you are angry with someone, learn to talk it out. You will be pleasantly surprised at how much better you will feel.

4) Get Rid of the Source of Your Frustrations

Some things in life cannot be changed and we need to live with them. On the other hand, there are often things that make us angry on an almost daily basis that, if we thought about them a bit, we could change them. We owe it to ourselves to do what we can to create situations in which we will feel less annoyed and angry. It is surprising to me, as a psychologist, to see many people who perpetuate a chronic state of frustration.

If you find yourself getting angry again and again in a particular situation, it might be time for you to make some changes.

For example, one women had to see her physician every three months to have her medication monitored. She found that she almost always has to wait between two and three hours in his office, even though her appointment was scheduled well in advance. She spoke to him about it on several occasions but the situation remained the same. Constantly irritated and frustrated, she decided to do something about the problem. After making several inquires among her friends, she found a physician who has an office that is better organized.

5) Harness All That Energy

When we are angry, we are in fact, energized and mobilized for action. All too often, this wonderful burst of energy that anger gives us gets disappointed and washed in fussing, fuming, gossip and sarcasm.

Anger not harnessed is a waste of a valuable natural psychological resource. Used properly, anger can be a force that can make our world more just and a better one to live in. Consider some of the positive things that were born of anger which were channeled in effective directions.

Three decades ago, Rosa Parks, an African-American in the South, got so angry at the humiliation of having to surrender her seat on the bus to a white man after a hard day's work – refused! Her action helped to spark the civil rights movement, which eventually resulted in removing the frame of enforced racial segregation in our country.

Two decades ago, a mother in Los Angeles, furious at the senseless killing of her daughter by a drunk driver, helped found the organization MADD, which has succeeded in raising the national drinking age and has helped to get tough laws in place to get drunken drivers off the road. As a result, hundreds of lives have been saved.

Most recently, families of new mothers, horrified at insurance companies insistence of "drive-through" deliveries, lobbied successfully so that, in most areas, at least a 48-hour stay is mandated

Are you angry at something?? GOOD!!

Get to your desk and write to your legislator, join an organization that will work for social change and justice, do something constructive with your anger! It would be shame to waste such a potentially powerful force that would make everyone's life a bit better.

Cutting the Jealousy Dragon Down To Size

"Sara has gotten that partnership that she wanted. Well good luck to her. I hope that she doesn't work herself to death."

"Bob and Jane just bought that new house. I don't know what they need three acres for — but that's their business."

"There were over 300 people at the wedding. It must have cost a year's salary. There was so much going on it felt like a zoo."

"Marcia's son, Phil, will probably be valedictorian this year — I'm glad our kid isn't a nerd."

"Yes, Lindsay is going out with Joe again. Just because he's the captain of the football team, he thinks he's so cool. I don't know that he sees in her — but I suspect she's doing things on the second date that I wouldn't do until I'm engaged. You know what I mean!"

Five different people, five different situations. One common theme. JEALOUSY!

In all the spectrum of human feelings, jealousy is the feeling that we are usually the most ashamed of. We tend to deny we are jealous, we rationalize away our comments and often stuff our feelings deep down into our minds. Out of sight, however, does not mean out of mind. Unaware of our feelings of envy, the jealousy monster pops out in unexpected ways and at unexpected times.

Green is the color most associated with sickness; *green* is also the color most associated with jealousy. I don't believe for a moment, that is just an idle coincidence. Indeed, jealousy, like sickness, can weaken us and corrode our very inner being.

Jealousy can be a most damaging and corrosive emotion. Great thinkers throughout the ages have recognized the damage that jealousy can do to our relationships with others; but, most of all, what jealousy can do to our own state of health and happiness. The Bible Story of Solomon tells us that "jealousy is a cruel as the grave." Many centuries later Dryden made a similar observation when he wrote "jealousy is the jaundice of the soul."

What are some of the causes of this very powerful human feeling?

On the most profound level the roots of jealousy can find their origins in our early childhood experiences. Psychologists know that a young child is completely egocentric. With an in-complete understanding of the world, the young child sees himself as very vulnerable – as well as very powerful. If, for example, a young child is angry at his father because his father refused him a cookie, and his father gets into an automobile accident that evening, the child sees the accident as being his fault. If the child becomes concerned about his mother's health, he might develop little private, magical rituals in order to safeguard her health. You all, I'm sure, remember the formula that would keep your mother healthy; "step on a crack, break your mother's back."

During this period, if a sibling is born, the child may feel unloved if his mother nurses the new baby. The feelings of anger and rejections soon become twisted together and a jealous stew begins to brew.

Later on as the child grows, there are inevitable blows to self-esteem as the realization dawns that other people can sometimes do things better – and they receive more attention. If someone grows up feeling that they can't do many things well, their self – esteem is low and jealous feelings proliferate and expand.

A couple of years ago I was consulted by a 42-year-old man whose marriage was nearly on the rocks of divorce because of his excessive and incessant jealousy.

Married for 12 years there were two fine children, a beautiful home and a wife who was faithful in every way. He had always exhibited some jealousy, but during the past two years, his jealousy became pathological. He wanted to know where she was every hour. And in the evening, she had to account for all of her time. When they would go out socially he would accuse her of paying too much attention to the other couple, even though they were friends for years. The final straw that nearly wrecked the marriage was when the wife found out, by accident that he had set up a device in the attic to "bug" the family phone.

Realizing that this was now pathological, she gave him the choice of going to a psychologist or a divorce lawyer. He chose to go to a psychologist. In working with him, I learned that he had grown up in the shadow of an extremely successful older brother. As a child his brother always did better in school, at sports, and socially. Although his parents tried to be even-handed, it was clear that they frequently were delighted with his older brother's successes.

When my patient left home to go to college he began to emerge out of the cocoon of his family situation. He did well in school, made friends, and for the first time in his life, began to feel good about himself. His self-esteem improved even more when, after college, he found an excellent job and eventually he established his own successful business.

While he was doing well financially, his jealousy subsided somewhat and he and his wife got along reasonably well.

Following a series of financial set backs that nearly resulted in bankruptcy, the patient's jealousy became intensified until it led to the events that precipitated the marital crisis. After working with him for a while, it became clear that his business failure deeply shook his self-confidence and it re-invoked all manner of old feelings of lack of worth. When he began to address the real issues of his self-doubts, the "jealousy dragon" retreated back into its cove and would emerge less frequently.

The seeds of jealousy often sprout in the soil of anger and frustration. One woman, for example, was known by all her friends as an acerbic jealous person, who all too frequently, would make jealous comments about the people she knew. She would denigrate their possessions, criticize their clothing and children, and like nothing more then to hear a "juicy" tidbit of malicious gossip which she could then spread about. Her jealous behavior caused considerable friction with her friends and family and, because of her actions, her system of social support began to shrink.

Underlying her jealous, often ugly behavior was a deep sense of frustration and anger. In high school, she was extremely gifted, and won a scholarship to a prestigious college in New England. After her sophomore year, her mother became ill and she returned home to care for her. When her mother died, she began to care for her father who was emotionally disabled. She took a job that she hated. Shortly after, she got married and remained home caring for the children. On the surface, she did all of the "right" things, but on a deeper level, she was angry and frustrated. She craved intellectual stimulation but harbored a deep resentment at never finishing her college degree.

The "jealousy monster" also feeds and nourishes by a sense of being ignored; a longing for affection and an exaggerated sense of competition.

Almost all human beings get greenish tinge from time to time, but if you find that tinge deepening into an "emerald green," it might be time to do some constructive work on yourself. Here are some of the things you can do to help cut the dragon down to size:

1) OK – So You're Jealous:

Perhaps the very first step in dealing with jealousy, is to own up to the fact that you are, indeed, jealous!

Many people have no difficulty in spotting and identifying jealousy in others. Like bad breath, however, it's easier to spot the problem in others, but not in ourselves. If we know that we have bed breath, we can floss our teeth, use a mouthwash or scrape our tongue. In a like manner, if we know that we are jealous, we can begin to take corrective measures.

It is hard to see our faults and some of us are too proud to admit that we even have them. We are all human, and to be human is to be imperfect.

Margaret, a married women, age 37, began to have increasingly difficult times with her younger sister. She had always enjoyed a good relationship but recently found that she was finding fault with her. She also realized that almost everything her sister did became a source of annoyance.

During a period of healthy introspection, Margaret came to the realization that her feelings towards her sister began to change shortly after her sister and her husband purchased a large house in a lovely neighborhood. Margaret had always felt she wanted a bigger home, but as yet, was unable to afford the house she wanted. As she became aware of her envy, she was able to cope with her jealousy in a less destructive manner.

2) Does The World Really Owe Me Anything?

As a nation, Americans are indeed blessed with a life of abundance. Today, the vast majority of us (unfortunately not everyone) live a lifestyle that was beyond the imagination of anyone 100 or 200 years ago. This lifestyle, to which we have easily become accustomed, is the dream of millions of people around the world who risk their lives trying to enter the Promised Land of the United States.

Our supermarkets have a variety of foods from around the world. Many of us have our own comfortable automobile which takes us where we care to drive. Our homes are cool in the summer heat and warm during the chill of winter. We have access to wonderful antibiotics that take away the pain of strep throat in 24 hours. Broken legs can be fixed and even damaged hearts can sometimes be mended. Each year our life expectancy rises. Only 100 or so years ago, our average life span was about 40 years. Today, it is almost double that.

We live in the kind of luxury that even great kings and monarchs would find unbelievable. Only 120 years ago!!

After a day's work, we can retire to our living room (or even a special room designed for this purpose) and, on a magical screen, access the entire world. We can entertain ourselves with symphony concerts or laugh at comedy. We can attend the funeral of English Princesses and a few days later have a front seat at the funeral of a remarkable nun halfway around the world in India. We can see news as it happens and watch championship tennis match from a better vantage point then we would have than if we were actually there.

Unhappily this very wonderful way of life has a dark side that gives us the subtle message that if we don't have the "latest" and the "newest" and the "best" (you fill in the blanks with "auto," "computer," "house," "plumbing," etc.) we somehow are missing out on the good life and we are falling behind in the race for the better life. This atmosphere promotes a sense of entitlement in the person that creates problems, not only for the person, for but for everyone around him/her.

A sense of "entitlement" is often an attitude that the person is completely unaware of until it triggers an acute jealousy attack. So the next time you feel yourself turning a little green, ask yourself "does the world really owe me anything?"

3) All That Glitters is Not Gold!

Jealous people have the bad habit of maximizing their own liabilities at the same time that they maximize the assets of others. Like any habit, this kind of thinking can become repetitive and almost automatic. Like a door that opens when someone walks into the path of an electric eye, the gate to the jealous dragon's cave lifts up to invite you in when the envious feelings begin to brew because you see someone with something you would like to have.

Admiration of something can often turn into envy and, indeed, this is a very human trait. Because of the universality of this kind of thinking, superstitious people in many different cultures live in fear of the "evil eye."

In the last analysis, the "evil eye" is a recognition that if we have something that is greatly admired or wanted by someone else, these jealous feelings can turn to thoughts of wishing us ill. And so, some people – wishing to protect themselves from the harm, instilled upon them by jealousy – will "knock on wood," wear "horns" around their neck or tie red ribbon on the baby carriage.

To cut your own pangs of jealousy down to a proper size, it is important to realize that all that glitters is certainly not gold. We never know, from just superficial glance, what problems or issues may exist under a surface of pleasant glitter.

There is the very ancient Greek myth that the Gods, tiring of the complaints that the mortals below were making about their individual bundle of troubles, decided to teach a lesson. According to this myth, everyone was able to put down their own bundle of troubles, and then would exchange it for the bundle of someone that they envied. Within a short time, there were great moans and cries as everyone wanted to get their own bundle of troubles back.

4) Broaden Your World – and Expand Your Interests!

Envy and jealousy are often fed by boredom and self-pity. Curiously, as someone's world narrows, little events enlarge and become monumental in proportion. If you read some of the diaries of prisoners of war who were held in solitary confinement, you can find descriptions of this kind of phenomenon.

One man, for example, imprisoned in solitary confinement for eight months, describes how the visit of an ant into the cell became an event of great importance. He observed the direction that the ant took. He watched the speed and marked the time of visit.

Under normal condition of activity and companionship, we would hardly be enthralled by the actions of an insect crawling up the wall. Under abnormal conditions of a lack of simulation, however, each small event becomes enlarged.

In a workplace situation where people are frustrated or poorly paid, jealous confrontations break out over tiny little details. Who gets the desk by the window? Who gets to use the fax machine first? Who didn't contribute to the coffee fund?

Henry Kissinger, observing the petty jealous behavior that sometimes exists in faculty situations on some campuses once remarked that the reason that these battles were so bitter was because the stakes were so low.

When jealous feelings begin to trouble you, a good antidote

is to push out the barriers of your narrow interests and broaden your view of the world. A new course, a visit to a museum, an afternoon volunteering your time, are activities that can work wonders.

5) Working – Not Wishing – Can Get You What You Want

Used wisely, jealousy can be of great help in clarifying our goals and values and can be a powerful spur to get us to where we really would like to be.

Donna, for example, found that she was snappy, gossipy and critical of two of her good friends. After thinking hard and honestly about her feelings, she came to the correct conclusion that her annoyance and anger was rooted in feelings of jealousy. Her jealousy, in turn, was focused on the considerable weight loss that her friends, Amy and Judy, had achieved during the past year.

In exploring this situation, Donna told me that she, Amy and Judy had made a New Year's resolution a year ago that they would try to lose some weight. All three of these women at the time felt that they were getting too heavy and they resolved to go on a program that would help them achieve their goal. One part of the program that they devised was to workout together at a local health club three times a week.

All went well for a month or two as all three friends began to lose weight. After six weeks or so, Donna began to find the routine boring and taxing and she soon began to find excuses when she didn't have time to exercise. Soon she didn't feel she needed to even make excuses – she just stopped.

When she thought about her situation rationally, she realized that Amy and Judy's success was due to lots of hard work. Deciding that putting up with the boredom and routine was worth it, she harnessed her feelings of jealousy and managed to convert and transform all this energy into some hard work.

Most physical trainers tell their students the hackneyed phrase "no pain – no gain." Indeed this aphorism can serve as a metaphor for lifting us out of a swamp of jealous feelings. If, for example, you want to lift a greater load, your muscles will be sore for a while. The soreness, however, is soon translated into growth and greater strength. One patient of mine, a few months ago, was a man who often felt a considerable amount of self-pity. A recreational runner who ran small distances, he frequently expressed many feelings of jealousy to some of his friends who had entered and completed marathons. One day, after expressing his envious feelings, his friend told him that if he, indeed, wanted to run a marathon, there were classes at the local runner's club that would prepare him for distance running and that he personally would run with him and help in his training. Reluctant and ambivalent at first, he overcame his inertia and entered the program. Two years later, he ran his first marathon (not breaking any speed records). Exhausted, yet elated, he told his wife "this was the happiest day of my life."

Jealous wishes can help us think about what we would like to have; but working is more likely to produce the results that we want.

CHAPTER 7

Ah, Loneliness!
All You Should Know and Do

Thomas Wolfe many years ago wrote, "The whole conviction of my life now rests upon the belief that loneliness, far from being a rare and curious phenomena, peculiar to myself and a few other solitary men, is the central and inevitable fact of human existence..."

As a practicing clinical psychologist, I know loneliness is not a respector of age or social position. Prince and pauper, young and old – all of use feel pangs of loneliness from time to time. Although loneliness has long plagued mankind, complaints about painful loneliness seem to have reached epidemic proportions.

In our mobile and rapidly changing society, many families are separated by miles. Other families, although living in close proximity to each other – even in the same house – are separated by generation or communication gaps. For all too many, America, in the last decade of the 20th century, has indeed become a lonely place.

The pain of loneliness may assume many forms. For some, it is experienced as a sharp sense of loss and isolation that can strike suddenly in the shower, the car or the supermarket. For others, loneliness is an ever-present shadow of emptiness that can darken one's spirits even in the midst of a joyous party.

To understand loneliness, it is important to remember that there is a big difference being alone and bring lonely. Aloneness occurs by choice – but loneliness contains the feeling of being involuntary.

All of us must spend some time alone if we are to expand our inner horizon, become aware of our deepest feeling or become involved in creative work.

Loneliness is the feeling that we experience when we are unwillingly separated from someone or something that we feel we need. Many people experience a painful bout of loneliness when they experience the loss of a loved one or through separation or death. Not handled properly, loneliness produced by such profound loss may undermine the person's health and very will to live.

Loneliness is also is also produced by an inability to handle rejection. A broken love affair, a lost friendship, a request for a promotion that is denied, can all be sparks that can ignite lonely feelings.

The weeds of loneliness are often fertilized by the false yet prevalent belief that happiness can only be achieved being surrounded by a mob of people. Bombarded by slick TV advertising, some people have come to view solitude as a social punishment that results from not using the proper mouthwash or the right deodorant.

Others, overly competitive, need to be "on top" all of the time. Having to "get the last word in" often results in alienation from others who resent being used as launching pads for personal ego trips.

One's self worth and security also play a powerful part in determining the need that you have for contact with others. When you feel frightened and unsure of yourself, you are more likely to turn towards other in search of comfort. Just as an exposed and isolated sheep becomes more vulnerable to being attacked by a predator, or cavemen ancestors learned to seek other of their kind in time of trouble.

Indeed, the very word, "gregarious" comes from the ancient Greek world that means herd or flock. In my work with troubled people, I have often found that underneath the facade of many overly gregarious adult, you can find a very frightened child.

In one classical experiment, Dr. John Darley demonstrated how needs for others increased in times of stress or fear. Working with college students, he observed that those students who feared participation in a psychological experiment were more likely to seek out contacts and conversations with students who were also waiting. Those students who were not afraid of the experiment, did not show as much need to socialize during the waiting period.

Emotionally healthy individuals are not afraid of self-confrontation that solitude almost always brings. Mature people often welcome brief respites from social contact so that they can come to terms with themselves. They use these precious periods of aloneness to "get it all together." Mature people also know that feelings of loneliness arise not so much from that quantity of social contacts that we have, but rather from the quality of our relationships and the very way that we live our lives.

In my work with people, I have learned that, if you know how to use periods of being alone in a constructive manner, you are indeed fortunate. If, however, you feel too lonely, here are some hints that many prove to be of help.

1) Be the First to Say Hello

Many lonely people often harbor feelings of hurt pride. They keep mental notes on "whose turn it is to call..." Fearing rejection, they often do not reach out to others lest they be rebuffed. Too often, they confuse another person's shyness with rejection.

In my years of clinical practice, I don't remember anyone who was put off by a friendly phone call, or an invitation to have coffee together.

A patient of mine, a lonely, shy, young engineer, learned much about how to deal with loneliness one afternoon when he was out-of-town on a business trip. Before his dinner meeting, he decided to have a swim. As he sat in his lounge chair sunning himself, he began to feel considerable self-pity because of his loneliness. His sense of being alone was intensified by the fact that there was a small group of "singles" about ten feet away who were laughing and talking. He wished that he could find an excuse to join with them. As he was stewing and fretting, he saw a young man approach the group. "Hello," he said. "My name is Fred Davis. I just arrived here this morning. I've never been to Phoenix before. Would you mind if I park my chair here while I go in for a swim?" After his swim, easy conversation began to flow and introductions and advice about Phoenix soon followed.

I know that when you are alone in an unfamiliar situation with strangers, it's natural to feel shy and a little afraid. It is tempting to protect ourselves by hiding behind a moat of aloofness and think walls of reserve. Sometimes these protective walls become too thick and the moat becomes too wide. When this happens, your fortress of self-prohibition can turn into a prison of loneliness.

When you become the first to say hello, you help to reassure the other person that you mean no harm. Do you know that a "stranger" is sometimes just a "friend" you haven't met a yet?

2) Make Friends with Yourself

Many lonely people simply do not know how to enjoy their own company. Feeling unworthy, the person who is not friends with himself/herself would never think of being nice to themselves. Some people can only affirm their own sense of worth by being in constant contact with others. Being alone unfortunately becomes confused with being a failure or being rejected.

People who are at odds with themselves feel martyred if they have to live alone temporarily or if they have to go to a movie by themselves. Not liking themselves, they treat themselves poorly. If they dine alone in a restaurant, they do so almost apologetically. They either rush through their meal or they use a newspaper or book to ward-off expected stares from others. Not being able to stand their own company, they assume that others will regard them as rejected outcasts who couldn't even find a companion for dinner. They begrudge themselves fun!

When you learn to accept yourself and begin to forgive your shortcomings, you can begin to become less dependent upon others.

It's human nature to want to share with others, but when it's not possible, we must learn to enjoy our own company. When we do so, we find that we have made a friend for life!

3) Let the Past Go

Used properly, memories of the past can nourish the present moment in the same way that last year's fallen leaves can fertilize a tree's present growth. Just the way excess mulch can stifle new growth instead of enriching the soil, covering over the present moment with excess memory can harm rather than heal.

One patient of mine, a bright vibrant woman of 53, spent most of her adult life caring for her four children. For years, her life was filled with visits to the dentist, PTA meetings and little league games. When her youngest daughter left for college, she felt herself descending into an almost unbearable pit of loneliness. She would walk through the empty rooms of her house and spend hours looking at old photographs and memorabilia of happier times.

When her husband would come home at night, he often

would find her sad and tearful. As her loneliness deepened, she became clearly depressed and entered treatment. After a few sessions, she became aware of how unproductive her dwelling in the past was. As she began to explore her life, she realized that she needed to become useful and needed.

She became a volunteer for "Meals on Wheels" and within a short period of time, the help that she brought to people lonelier than herself acted as an almost magical cure for her own loneliness.

4) Take a New Route Home

When people complain of being lonely, I often ask if they have done anything different lately. If they haven't, I often suggest that they begin to vary fixed patterns of behaviour in even small ways. Sometimes, I even suggest that when they drive home from my office, they take a different route.

Sometimes a painful bout of loneliness may mean that it is high time to change a pattern of behavior that has become routine and dull. One middle-aged dentist, for example, complained of painful feelings of loneliness. I initially found it difficult to understand why he should feel lonely. He had a happy marriage, two healthy kids and a busy practice. In addition, he was actively involved in several professional and social activities.

As I learned more about him, I found some clues that eventually helped to partially solve the mystery of his unhappiness. For the past fifteen years, he and his wife played bridge with the same group on Friday nights. Every last Wednesday of the month, he attended a Dental Association meeting and each year he took his family to the same summer resort during the first two weeks in August. Like a primitive Aztec calendar, his life proceeded in a predictable, orderly circle.

When he came to understand that much of his loneliness was rooted in boredom, he began to introduce some changes into his life. He attended a three-day workshop on improved office management that was sponsored by the American Dental Association and when he returned home, he updated some office procedures. He took a course in sculpting and he and his wife went to Europe last summer. Open to new experiences and new friendships, his clouds of loneliness were dispelled by the winds of gentle and gradual change.

5) Don't be So Much of a Conformist

Many who are lonely are not lonely because of lack of company but because they sacrifice their own unique feelings and ideas on an alter of needless conformity. There are many, who, although they are surrounded by thoughtful friends and loving families, still complain that they are lonely. These people are really not lonely for others but rather they are lonely for disowned parts of themselves.

All of us have to strike a healthy balance between our own needs and the needs of others. Those who care only for their own needs and disregard the feelings of others soon become irresponsible and selfish. Those who care only for the needs of others at the expense of their own desires, find themselves alienated from their own feelings. It is this sense of alienation that is soon experienced as loneliness.

Often, chronic "people pleasers" learn to suppress their own unique desires and in their efforts to please, soon hardly know what they truly want.

Our emotional needs are probably as unique as our fingerprints. Mike, for example, may have a strong need to read and learn. Phil, on the other hand, prefers more strenuous activities such as tennis or jogging, while Sarah longs to do some creative handiwork.

Recent research has indicated that a certain degree of important aspects of our personalities are probably rooted in our genetic structure and physiology.

To avoid a sense of loneliness and alienation, it is important to know who we are and what we want. Then, when we can learn to mesh our own needs and express them in a socially acceptable and harmless manner, we're on the road to banishing loneliness.

6) Learn to Cherish Solitude

When you practice using your time "alone" constructively, you often no longer have time to feel lonely. If you find yourself overly dependent on the company of others, try spending at least two hours a week alone – voluntarily.

The famous American writer Henry David Thoreau once wrote "I never found the companion that was so companionable as solitude. We are, for the most part, lonely when we go about among men then when we stay in our chambers!"

The wise and kindly Thoreau knew that when you choose to be alone, temporary periods of enforced solitude will no longer seem to be so unbearable.

When you are alone, try to channel some of that precious solitude into constructive activity. Painting, writing, making a needed home repair or baking homemade bread can give you a sense of accomplishment and restore your sense of self-esteem.

Every one of us have had periods in which we feel lost in the barren desert of loneliness but by working for others and by helping others more lonely than ourselves, we need not become permanent inhabitants in a wasteland of despair.

To find our own path, we might well remember the advice of John Kennedy who wrote, "Every man can make a difference and every man should try."

PART THREE

Family &
Communication

CHAPTER 8

Your Family and How You Communicate

"*I told him to take the garbage out at least 20 times – Guess what? It's still in the kitchen!*"

"*She came home with a pretty new sweater. I asked her casually 'How much did it cost?' Before I knew it she went nuts.*"

"*I'm really upset about my daughter's new boyfriend; so when my husband came home I asked him to speak to her about him. All of a sudden, it was World War III.*"

If you are like most people I know, there may be times when you just can't seem to get your message across to family members. Even worse, a message that you send becomes misunderstood or garbled.

Psychologists know that communication is the tool that can make or break a family. Effective communication between family members can open up channels of understanding and love. Conversely, poor communication skills can silt over and clog channels of affection and trust.

Study after study has demonstrated that effective communication is the *single most important* factor in marriage and one of the *most important* factors in effective parenting. In one study, two groups of married couples were videotaped. The first couple described themselves as happily married and the second group viewed themselves as unhappily married.

After these couples interacted with each other for a period of time, the video tapes were carefully observed. It was noted that the happily married couple, in contrast to the unhappily married couple, spoke *more directly* to each other; they *showed more eye contact* and they often gave *feedback after their partner spoke.*

It can be surmised that happily married couples know how to communicate better than unhappily married couples.

In my work with families, I have observed both helpful as well as terribly destructive communication patterns. I have seen communications that fix and heal and others that hurt and alienate. If you are interested in improving your communication in your own family, here are some tips I know can help a lot.

1) Listen, Really Listen

It's amazing to me in my work with couples and families to observe how few people really listen to the other person who is talking. Often, we are so busy planning to get our own point across that we fail to hear what the other person is saying. Listening well is an even more important part of communication than talking.

In many ways, human beings are alone. We all exist in a private world of hopes, dreams, disappointments and fears. When we learn to listen well to another who is trying to let us into their own private world, we build a bridge that can span the gap between two people.

Recently, I worked with a family who was concerned about the fact that their daughter, a senior in high school, wasn't working on her college applications. Each time she began to give excuses for her delay, her mother or father would interrupt by giving her "parent advice" with comments such as "that's just an excuse – there's nothing more important now than getting out your applications."

Had they listened more carefully and attentively, they would have come to realize that their daughter's delay in sending out applications was based on her deep fear that she would be rejected.

Listening, really listening, is the essence of much psychotherapy. Several years ago, I saw a woman for a session. She was very anxious and spoke "nonstop." In fact, even if I wanted to, I couldn't have slipped in a word. After 45 minutes, at the close of the session, she said, "Thank you doctor, you really helped me figure it all out!"

When we listen, we need to pay attention not only to verbal communication but to nonverbal communication as well. A tapping finger often indicates anger; a tapping foot perhaps indicates a desire to leave; widely dilated eyes suggest interest.

I often tell people who communicate poorly that God gave us two ears and one mouth. Do you think that this means that to have good communication we need to listen twice as often as we talk? I do!!!

2) Remember, the Other Person isn't a Mind-Reader!

When we communicate with someone else, it is important to send a message that is clear. You can't expect someone to know something unless you tell them what you want them to know.

One of the most common "hang-ups" in family communication results from expecting the other person to know what we want or feel without us telling them.

One couple I saw recently had the following conversation:

She: "I'm really mad about our anniversary. I know you took me to a nice restaurant, but you know how much I wanted to go into the city and see a Broadway show."

He: "If you wanted to go to see a show to celebrate, why didn't you ask me?"

She: "If you really cared about me and understood me, I wouldn't have to ask – you would know!"

This, "if you loved me, I wouldn't have to ask" scenario is seen by family therapists regularly. As people progress in their communication skills, most come to realize that we can't expect someone else to be a mind-reader. Frequently, even if we don't play the "mind-reader" game blatantly, we do so in a more subtle way. One of the most useless speech fillers is the phrase "you know."

One young woman was trying to communicate to me her problems with her boyfriend. Anxious and upset, her speech went something like this: "He called and the conversation got heated, you know. I told him that he couldn't treat me like, you know. When he hung up on me, I felt like, you know!"

Carefully and gently, I explained to her that "No – I don't know." I could only guess her feelings. As she calmed down and became more explicit by verbalizing her feelings and thoughts, I was able to understand her more fully.

3) Get Rid of the Third Party

One of the common characteristics of families that are having problems is that they don't send messages directly – they do so by a third party.

The pattern of "putting someone in the middle" creates more problems not only for the people who are trying to communicate, but even more so for the "middleman." Family therapists call this form of communication "triangulation."

Triangulation typically occurs when a couple are angry at each other and they start to send messages through one of the children.

Father: "Tell your mother to pass the salt."

Mother: "Tell your father that I'll pass the salt if he stops hogging the pepper."

Often, the child who gets caught in such a triangle becomes symptomatic and develops all manners of psychological problems.

An angry divorce where the child is put in the middle can be especially distressing. One teenage boy, whose parents were not talking to each other during their separation and divorce, told me, "I don't think I can stand it anymore. I feel like a message boy – 'tell your mother this' or 'tell your father that.' The only time I feel halfway decent is when I'm high. I know that pot is no good for you – but it makes me feel good."

Remember the game of "telephone" you played as a child? In "telephone" the first kid passes a message to the second kid who passes it on to the third and so on. By the time the message gets to the last player, everyone laughs at how garbled and distorted the message becomes. Funny as a game, but not so funny in real life.

Like real life telephones, if we dial directly, we are much less likely to get a wrong number.

4) Don't Argue with Feelings

A sure fire way of jamming a communication is to argue with someone else's feelings.

A few months ago, I was working with a troubled high school boy who was unhappy about a multitude of adolescent issues. He had been cut from the soccer team, his friends didn't include him when they took a trip to the shore *and* he was having trouble with his history teacher.

During a family session, he tentatively expressed these feelings and disappointments to his parents. His father's response was, "You're making a big thing out of nothing. High school is the *happiest time* of your life. If you're not happy now, I don't know if you'll ever be happy."

The boy's response to this was to stop talking. He looked ashamed and angry. The next day, I received a phone call that he had run away.

Feelings are not like faucets. You can't turn them on or off. When we begin to argue with someone's feelings, it usually signals the end of the communication. When we acknowledge someone else's feelings, we can then begin to get our message across. Had the parents of this young man accepted the fact that he was in an unhappy patch in his life, all of them might have come to some constructive solutions to his emotional distress.

5) If You Say It too Loud or too Strong, You Might Not be Heard at All

All of us, as we deal with the vicissitudes of life, develop mechanisms of defense that protect us from psychological threats and changes. When we feel threatened, we automatically throw up a protective barrier around ourselves to defend against the perceived threat. Like a turtle who, sensing danger, retreats in to his shell, we close up and tend to shut out the outside world.

Most of us are more likely to hear a message when it is presented in a calm, straightforward and logical manner. Screaming, shouting and yelling may grant us some temporary release of our frustration and anger. In the long run, a message that is sent in this fashion is much less likely to be heard.

6) Give Some Feedback!

To keep communication going, we have to give some feedback to let the other person know that their message is received. If we don't give something back to the sender, communication comes to a grinding halt.

The feedback that we give has to let the sender of the message know that we understand – or least that we are trying to understand – what they are trying to communicate to us. All too often, the channels of communication get shut down because we give no feedback – or worse – we give feedback that ends the conversation.

A few months ago, a couple with marital difficulties were in my office. The wife was deciding whether or not she would leave her present job to take another position that offered more money but which required a long commute. She was discussing her alternatives, but before she was able to sort them all out, her husband replied, "It's clear that you should stay where you are!" At that point, communication verbally ceased. When you give feedback, avoid the temptation to play "judge".

When you give a quick verdict about someone else's dilemma, you are almost always guaranteed that your verdict will be appealed and often overthrown.

The late psychologist Carl Rogers and his followers developed a helpful technique called "reflecting back."

A typical example of "reflecting back" goes something like this:

He: How has your day been?

She: The car wouldn't start and I had to get it jump-started. I got a call from school that Jimmy has been acting up again and the vet said the dog will need an operation.

He: Wow! It's like everything happened to you all at once. You sound like you've been through the mill!

This kind of feedback encourages communication and verbal resolution of the problem. Imagine what would have happened if he had responded to his wife's distress by saying, "Too bad – I had a rough day also."

Good communication with other family members doesn't just happen. But with a little bit of practice and awareness, you can make things better.

CHAPTER 9

The Five Myths
Of Marriage

O nce upon a time, in a country called the United States, there was a lovely lady and a marvelous man who loved each other so much that they decided to marry. After a short while, two healthy children were born. They became a family.

But, after the children came, problems began to multiply. When the children started school, the problems got even worse. The marvelous man thought that his son should enter kindergarten early so that he could make up a year. The lovely lady thought that he needed the year to mature. Soon, the lovely lady became a "loud" lady and the marvelous man became a "mean" man.

When their daughter was in junior high school, the "not-so-lovely-anymore" lady thought that their daughter should not be allowed to hang out with a group of kids who seemed to have too much freedom. The "not-so-marvelous-anymore" man thought that the daughter needed to make her own choices.

When both children were in high school, the parents were

shocked to learn that their son had been smoking pot and their daughter decided not to go to college. The once-upon-a-time lovely lady blamed her husband, and the once-upon-a-time marvelous man blamed his wife. Disagreements became arguments. Arguments became battles. Both felt angry, confused, resentful and cheated.

Consequently, they both went to lawyers (it's not important who went first) and they officially registered their unhappiness by getting a divorce.

I wish I could tell you that the above story was only a fable but, unhappily, it is true.

For some lucky people, the family seems a safe container that is enclosed by invisible walls of love and concern. In such a family, an individual can replenish a diminished sense of self-esteem or can receive help in healing the uninvited physical and emotional wounds that occur in the process of living and growing. For all too many people, the family, instead of being a container of support and love, becomes a crucible of conflict in which old problems boil and scald as family members shrink rather than grow as they get hurt rather than healed.

As a practicing psychologist who often works with families, I am impressed by the fact that most parents try their very best to help their children grow into happy and healthy adults. These good efforts are often thwarted by false information and mistaken beliefs about family living. All too often, faulty facts foul up families. While there are a lot of phony beliefs that can make for problems, here are five fables that I find to be particularly destructive.

Myth 1: Children Can Be Our Second Chance

Whether we realize it or not, every time a child is born, he or she becomes the immediate heir of all our unfulfilled dreams, thwarted ambitions and the potential repairer of all our disappointments. In the award-winning Rodger and Hammerstein's musical "Carousel," Billy Bigilow sings of his dreams for his yet unborn son in the song that begins with the words, "My boy Bill will be tall and as strong as a tree..."

In American society, with our democratic notion that everyone has an opportunity to become president or at least to live a life that is more satisfying than our own, the burden of parental unfulfilled dreams and ambitions can become particularly heavy.

We are lucky if we can identify and articulate the dreams we have for our kids. Most of the time, many of these dreams and fantasies are unconscious. Without awareness, therefore, many parents don't even realize that they have been pushing and pulling their growing child into a "Procrustian" mold cast from their own unrealized dreams and ambitions.

In a famous study conducted a few years ago, two psychologists interviewed more than 1,000 little league football players. *None* of the parents interviewed in the study believed that they had pressured their children into playing football. More than a quarter of the children – in their own interviews – said that they joined because of parental pressure.

When we try to impose our dreams on our children and unconsciously urge them to fulfill our frustrated desires, a psychological disaster awaits. Kids have the unfortunate habit of dreaming their own dreams. When their dreams for themselves collide with our dreams for them – watch out!

A few years ago, for example, I saw a woman who was delighted with her daughter's new fiancé. He came from the right school, had the proper pedigree and was, with all that, a nice guy.

When the young couple planned their wedding, they wanted a small backyard family affair, a small dinner and a month long honeymoon in Europe. My patient began to urge her daughter to have a larger affair. Arguments ensued. The daughter and her fiancé conceded almost every one in order to "make Mom happy."

Suffice to say within six months, the small backyard wedding expanded into a planned reception for over 250 guests ("After all, dear, they are our good friends").

After the daughter lost battle after battle, the final explosion came after her mother insisted that she purchase silk matchbook covers with the names and date of the wedding to be placed on each table. Daughter and fiancé finally said, "Absolutely not! We hate those things!" In spite of protest, the matchbooks were delivered five weeks before the wedding. Guess what happened?! The young couple went to Las Vegas and got married there. All the plans for the big wedding were canceled.

In helping this woman sort out her feelings, it became clear where the push for the big wedding originated. When she got married, during World War II, she wanted to marry her fiancé before he was to be shipped overseas to an uncertain fate. With no time to plan for a wedding, they hastily put together an informal family dinner. Years later, even though she was happy with her marriage, she nursed unconscious feelings of having been cheated. In attempting to impose her desires on her daughter, a potential happy family event was turned into a minor tragedy.

Are you aware of what dreams you are trying to impose upon your kids?

Myth 2: Parents Are Solely Responsible for a Child's Behavior

A couple of years ago, I was consulted by a conscientious couple terribly distraught over their 7-year-old son's behavior. In school, he was restless, distractible, and would often call out in class. At home, he was oppositional, negative and sometimes abusive to his 4-year-old sister. With his friends, he was bossy, irritating and aggressive.

When this couple told me about their son, it was clear that

THE FIVE MYTHS OF MARRIAGE

they were both angry and guilty. Husband blamed wife for being too indulgent. Wife blamed husband for being too strict. Each blamed themselves for not having been able to control the boy's behavior in a better manner.

I agreed to see the child for an evaluation and my testing suggested to me that this boy, in all probability, had some neurological and perceptual impairment. After the evaluation, I recommended that the child be seen by a pediatric neurologist. The neurologist confirmed my suspicions. When the child was placed on the appropriate regimen of medication and behavioral management, his behavior at school, at home and in the neighborhood improved markedly.

A few generations ago, children who had conduct problems were seen as simply being "bad apples." Not too long later, almost every problem that a child had was blamed on poor or inadequate parenting. In recent years, we have learned that genetic and physical factors play an important role in helping to determine the behavior of a child just as much as environmental influences.

Some studies: (1) Adopted children's rate of alcoholism is closer to the rate of their biological rather than their adoptive parents. (2) Many personality traits seem to be consistent throughout the life span. (3) Identical twins separated at birth often show a marked similarity in behaviors and personality even though they were raised in different homes.

Today, most knowledgeable researchers believe that behavior is determined both by heredity as well as environment.

So, before you blame yourself for a child's problem, try and find out what may be causing it and then fix what you can and accept those things that you may not be able to fix.

Myth 3: One Family Member is Exactly Like Another

"I know exactly what you're going through," said a mother

to her teenage daughter when she saw her fretting. "When I was your age, I also was worried about my weight. You're just like me you know..."

"I'm not worried about my weight, I'm worried about Penny who is getting into drugs."

No one individual is exactly like any other individual. Even identical twins raised in the same household differ from each other in many important ways.

Sometimes, if a child looks like or acts in a similar way as another family member, we identify that child with another person and make the mistake of attributing all of that person's characteristics onto that child. Often, if we think we know all about the person, we share our thoughts and fears out loud.

Sometimes, these verbalized fears serve to label the person in dangerous, destructive ways. One teenage boy I saw several years ago was getting into some brushes with the law for stealing. On one occasion, he took some gum from a check-out counter in a supermarket; in another, he tried to walk out of a drugstore with a package of ball-point pens.

I learned that when he was seven years old, he took a baseball that belonged to a friend (Experimenting with taking things that don't belong to us is not uncommon behavior in six or seven year olds).

His mother overreacted badly. She punished him severely and kept telling him as she lectured, "You're just like your Uncle Mike. We won't have this kind of behavior in this house."

I learned from her, when I saw her privately, that she had a younger brother, Mike, who was the "shame of the family." He began as a juvenile delinquent and by the time he was 25, he was serving time in the state penitentiary.

When I got to know the boy better and asked him about his stealing, he replied, "I don't know exactly why I do it, but I guess it's because I'm just like my Uncle Mike."

Watch out when you tell Pete that he is just like Uncle Joe or Sarah that she is just like Cousin Louise. By saying it, you might just make it happen.

Myth 4: A Good Family Rarely has Conflicts

In my work with families, I know that each family unit is really a unique system of relationships that are constantly changing and shifting. Love and hate are, indeed, closely related and ebb and flow within family systems like the tide of life itself. Family conflicts are the way that people begin to signal their need to renegotiate their differences.

All too often, our picture of a happy family is of a mother, father and two children (a boy and a girl, of course!) heading down to Florida to "do" Disney World. On the way, they sing verses of "Row, Row, Row Your Boat ...", in time of course.

Real families just don't act like that. In the real world, Jeremy fights with Marge over whose turn it is to sit next to Daddy and later on, when they stop for lunch, Marge complains that Jeremy had one more French fry than she did.

Psychologists know that sibling rivalry, with all of its unpleasant bickering and complaining, seems to be a necessary part of growing up. Hopefully, out of these conflicts, children eventually learn to assert themselves, to have a sense of self-esteem and eventually to share.

If the conflict is too severely suppressed or forbidden, these lessons may never be learned. One teenage girl I saw was severely depressed. When I saw her parents for the initial interview, they proudly told me that, "Everyone in the family gets along so well – we aren't like those families who argue all the time – we can't understand why Janice is so unhappy all the time."

As I got to know Janice better, it became clear that much of her unhappiness was related to the fact that the "family gets along so well." Everyone in the family grouping was afraid of any conflict or anger and so Janice was truly sitting on a powder keg of unexpressed anger that was in danger of "imploding."

Janice had many feelings of resentment towards her brother who seemed to be clearly favored by her father. She also felt that she was treated unfairly in her mother's demands to know all about her friends and her ongoing comparison of their grades with those of Janice.

As Janice began to express her feelings, there initially was annoyance and arguments. After a period of time, Janice was finally "heard" and her parents' behavior towards her began to change. When this occurred, Janice began to experience some relief from her emotional distress.

Every healthy family has conflicts and disagreements. The trick is to learn how to air and share these differences in a healthy, non-destructive way.

Myth 5: Children Hold a Marriage Together

It wasn't so long ago that when marital conflict began to erupt in a family, the folk-wisdom that was given to the family said, "Have a child – there's nothing that can help an ailing marriage like a new marital interest in a child." *WRONG!! VERY WRONG!!*

In my clinical experience, I often observe that in some ways, children are the natural enemies of marriage. Rather than holding a marriage together, having children puts an additional strain on a marriage and the stress that having children inevitably brings may prove to be the last straw for a relationship.

My own observation is supported by solid research from studies of marital happiness.

In one such study, for example, hundreds of married couples were questioned about the degree of marital happiness and contentment that they experienced. This study (as well as others) found that the greatest degree of marital happiness occurred during the earliest stage of marriage. As children arrived and began to grow, the reported rate of marital happiness began to steadily decline. Happiness began to improve once again after all of the children left home.

Unless one's own emotional problems are faced, recognized and worked through, the arrival of a new child causes these problems to "heat up." When the heat gets too intense, everyone in the family can get scalded.

Having a baby is fairly easy. Raising a healthy, competent child in our complicated society is a daunting task and certainly *NOT* one for emotional sissies!

CHAPTER 10

Marriage American Style:
Ethnicity, Family Backgrounds and Other Sources of Conflict

DEAR DR. SUGARMAN: "My wife and I have been married for about six years, but something keeps cropping up that's been a problem for us: The families we come from – what I mean is – both of us come from strong family backgrounds (both our parents are still together, both prosperous, and we have close siblings). My wife and I are in our early 30s and we had our first child two years ago. But, even now our disagreements are about the values we came from: The way we were raised is beginning to conflict with how we are raising our two-year-old. We're both Catholic (she's Italian – I'm Irish), so its not as if there are huge differences in our backgrounds. How much of this is normal? How much do family backgrounds get in the way of being happy in your own marriage?"

Long Question – Short Answer – A LOT!!

In recent years, psychological research has found that our family backgrounds are crucial to our happiness (or lack thereof) in our marriage. Family therapists know (even if the newly married couple doesn't) that the marital bed – besides husband and wife – is shared by the ghostly influence of his and her families.

By now, almost everyone knows how much better (statistically) is the prognosis for a marriage if both "he" and "she" come from stable, happy homes in which they both observed and learned techniques for making a happy marriage. Not as many people are aware of how important the more subtle cultural factors that can create misunderstanding and conflict.

In recent years, the slowly bubbling "melting pot" that is a proud and unique aspect of American culture has heated up to a virtual boil as people from different cultural backgrounds meet, talk, fall in love and get married. Second generation Italian-Americans marry first generation Germans, Greeks marry Norwegians and, in increasing numbers, Catholics, Protestants and Jews are marrying each other. Even interracial marriage, once highly unusual, is more common. All too often, this rapid blending of cultures, if not appreciated and understood by a couple, can produce – instead of delightful diversity – divisive difficulty.

Just the way that the last thing fish would be aware of is the water that surrounds them – so most people are not consciously aware of how the culture in which we are raised surrounds every aspect of our life. This culture largely determines the language that we speak, how we express our emotions, our attitudes towards others, political views, ideas of what the good life is all about and more.

To make it even more complicated, our culture and its values are changing at an accelerating rate. Take our attitudes toward children, for example: Many may not know that up until 200 years or so ago, children were routinely beaten, disregarded or often killed at birth (mostly if they were girls). In fashionable circles, breastfeeding was regarded as a menial, annoying task. In 1780, the police chief of Paris estimated that the majority of babies born in Paris that year were sent away to live with wet nurses until they were weaned.

As recently as 70 years ago, the American attitude was that children needed firm and harsh discipline, spankings and punishment lest they become "spoiled." No time-outs and no surfing the Net for hours to find "Tickle-Me Elmo" dolls.

When we get married and start a new family, we carry with us all the old cultural baggage, both positive and negative, that we have accumulated through the years as well as new baggage that arises from our rapidly changing value system.

Many couples that I see are caught somewhere between "Leave it to Beaver" and "Beavis and Butthead." Both parents working, instead of being an oddity is now almost the norm. Daycare, once rare, is usual. But, and here's the big but, many couples often feel guilty and torn as they make the cultural leap from their own families of origin to their new family of choice.

Cultural differences in a marriage often surface and become a problem when children arrive. In some ways, children are the "natural enemies" of marriage. As they grow, the value system of both husband and wife comes to the foreground as they begin to argue about "what is best" for little Joe or Josephine.

Studies of marital happiness reveal that marital satisfaction is greatest during two time periods. The first two years of marriage and then again after the children are grown and have left home. Many of these arguments, in the last analysis, merely represent attempts to impose or solve the cultural differences and conflict. It is important to gain some awareness of what you can do to have your own cultural differences become your friends rather than your foes.

1) Understand Where He/She is Coming From

Any marriage, particularly if it is a marriage between people from diverse backgrounds, represents somewhat of a cultural clash. Even if the marriage partner is from a very similar background, there are often subtle cultural differences that will exist. These cultural differences need to be understood and appreciated. If not, conflict and misunderstanding will often erupt.

A few years ago, for example, I worked with a couple having a bitter disagreement about visiting his mother. It seems that the last time they visited the husband's mother for dinner, she gave her granddaughter some wine to drink. The wife, horrified, felt that her mother-in-law was callous and uncaring and was acting in total disregard for the child's welfare. "She'll make the baby sick – she's only 3-years-old. What is she trying to do – make a drunk out of her?" the wife vehemently stated. "But it's only a taste of wine – what are you making a big deal about?" was the husband's retort. As they fought, it became obvious that they were in the middle of a *cultural misunderstanding.*

While they shared similar backgrounds – both were raised in New Jersey, both graduated from junior colleges and both were moderately observant Catholics – there were also some important cultural differences in their backgrounds that fueled the fires of their argument.

He was a second-generation Italian-American and she was first generation Irish-American. His parents were raised in a part of Italy in which wine was viewed as a nourishing food that in small doses would "put roses on the cheeks of the children." Her parents, in contrast, were raised in a part of Ireland where alcohol was seen as "spirits" and could only lead to alcoholism, conduct problems and sickness.

Had the wife been more aware of her husband's heritage, she would have realized that her mother-in-law's giving the child some wine was an act of love. If she indeed did not want her child to have any, the whole matter could have been handled in a calmer manner. So, as a very important first step in handling cultural differences, try to understand where he or she is coming from.

2) Understand Where You are Coming From

Just the way you need to know where he/she is coming from, you need to examine your own strongly held beliefs and family customs. What are the values that you hold dear? What are your beliefs about what are desirable behaviors in a marriage partner or a child? An honest "taking stock" can often pinpoint vital values that were part of your cultural heritage.

In a recent study, for example, residents of Hong Kong were asked how important certain traits would be for them when they chose a marriage partner. Those Hong Kong residents who grew up with a British background rated humor and sensitivity as most important. Others in this study, coming from a Chinese background, valued creativity and astuteness about managing financial affairs as being most important.

When you can identify the values that are most important to your marriage, you can avoid considerable conflict. One couple, for example, was frequently fighting about their child's behavior. She accused him of being harsh and mean, and he, in turn, felt that she was lackadaisical and uninterested in their child. When they came to examine their values, he started to realize that he felt the most important value that good parents could teach was discipline, while she stressed encouraging a child's creativity. Once these core values were identified, they were better able to resolve their differences.

3) Beware of Ethnocentricity

If there is one thing that ALL cultures have in common, it would be ethnocentricity. Social psychologists define ethnocentricity as the tendency to regard our own culture as being superior and our ways of doing things the "best" and "most civilized."

Up until recently, for example, the Chinese had two words for "man." One word referred to Chinese and the other word was reserved for non-Chinese individuals and was literally translated as "barbarian."

A healthy pride in our own cultural heritage is great but when our pride takes the form of arrogant superiority, ethnocentricity can began to cause many ugly interpersonal and inter-group tensions.

Like bad breath, we are quite aware of other people's ethnocentricity while we ignore our own. If we can, however, confront our own feelings of subtle superiority, we can come to understand and appreciate the cultural music that is part of a blended family that came from diverse cultural backgrounds.

4) You've Heard This One – Talk It Out

In marriage counseling, it has almost become a cliché to attribute a poor or failing marriage to poor communication. Cliché or not, problems with communication are at the root of many a marital problem. When a couple comes from different backgrounds, talking it out becomes vital. If she's a Baptist and he's a Catholic, to which church will the children go? If he's Jewish and she's a Mormon, will they have a Christmas tree, a menorah – or both?

Couples from different cultural backgrounds can succeed in making a meaningful and satisfying marriage if they put all the cards on the table and make joint decisions. In doing so, they need to talk about their feelings, hopes and resentments.

One couple, for example, was beginning to experience considerable friction. The wife came from a first-generation Greek-American family and he grew up in England and arrived in the states when he was about 20. They were very much in love, but after a few years of marriage, she became increasingly upset by his lack of outward display of emotions. She accused him of having ice water in his veins. He, in turn, became more and more annoyed by her frequent emotional displays. As they started to talk to each other in counseling session, he was able to explain to her that as a child at school in England, overt emotional displays were regarded as "unmanly" and, in fact, were seen as rude. She came to understand that he did indeed feel things deeply – but understated the expression of those feelings. In talking it out, he in turn learned that her overt expressions of emotion did not always mean that she was completely furious or distraught – but often – only an indication that she was mildly annoyed or frustrated.

In talking out problems that arise from cultural differences, it sometimes makes a lot of sense to "agree to disagree."

Agreeing to disagree can often make much more sense than endless arguing about the merits of one's case or continuously badgering our partner in a vain effort to convince them that our way is the best. One couple that I knew (she is American – he is an Indian from Bombay) both loved curry. He spent hours trying to teach her to enjoy heavily spiced curry. She kept arguing that, while she enjoyed curry, she couldn't tolerate so much spice. After a while, what was initially good-natured soon became annoying – until they agreed to disagree. Now when she prepares curry, she adds extra spice to his and very little to her own. This simple solution can be applied to cultural marital conflicts that are much more weighty than the proper way to prepare rice and chicken!

5) Pick and Choose and Make Your Own Traditions

Along with the problems of cultural differences, there are many blessings. Living with cultural diversity is like dining at a wonderful smorgasbord meal. You can pick some of this, try some of that and eventually you can pick and choose what you would like on your plate so you can be nourished and satisfied.

Many of our traditions come from very different cultures. Christmas trees probably came from Germany and Santa Claus from Holland. Some of the traditions we take for granted are not terribly old – and new traditions and customs gradually become adopted by many people.

In Mexico, for example, it was a common practice for people to light their pathways to their home with small candles on Christmas Eve. This tradition has now taken firm hold in the American Southwest and is enjoying increasing popularity each year in the rest of the country.

What a happy thing it is when a couple picks and chooses from their own traditions and cultures and even, at times, begin their own! One couple that I know who were tired of the excesses of Easter, now spend part of every Easter working in a homeless shelter. Now, their teenage children come along and some of their friends come to help. Another family, burned out by backyard barbecues and fireworks on July Fourth, began to take their children to a different museum on that day.

So, pick, choose, innovate, create and enjoy the wonderful cultural diversity that is a theme of our times!

CHAPTER 11

Seven Ways to Help Your Child in School

When Summer ends, the water skis, the cold drink cooler and the tents get stored once again in the attic. Untold numbers of new sneakers, pencils, pens and notebooks are purchased during August and the stores fill with preparations for Halloween and the kids are back in school.

At this time of year, most parents begin to worry a bit about how the school year will progress. Will Mark's new teacher send a note that complains about his lack of motivation and achievement? Will Sarah's teacher call about her late term papers? Will the principal call about Phil's daydreaming and poor conduct?

As a practicing clinical psychologist, I can tell you that a substantial number of referrals to psychologists are directly related to problems with school and learning. I have never, in my years in practice, met a parent who did not want their child to achieve in school. I do, however, constantly meet parents who, in spite of their dreams and the desires for their children's academic success, simply do not know what they can do to help achieve these goals.

If your child is doing well in school and achieving all that she/he might, you are lucky. If you are worried about the new academic year, here are a few tips that can help your child in school.

1) Become Involved

Almost all healthy children, from the time they are infants, long to please their parents. When it comes to school, perhaps the first and most important step that parents can take is to let their child know – by words and deeds – that school is important and that achievement counts.

In our busy society, parents often become preoccupied with business and financial problems. There are times when the house needs to be re-modeled or a new roof is needed. At other times, the five-year-old car has become unreliable and a new car is needed. The old boss may be tougher to work for and there's the possibility of taking a new job in Ohio. With all of these problems and decisions and concerns swirling around, it's no wonder that so many parents in subtle and sometimes not-so-subtle ways disengage from their child's schooling in spite of their deepest desires for their kids to do well in school.

One youngster I knew was in the fifth grade when her parents consulted with me because of her poor academic achievement and performance. She had done well in first and second grades, but in the third grade her performance began to decline. Her teachers all had the same comments. "Janice is very bright but she doesn't seem to care about school. She is much more involved with her friends and I find it hard to motivate her."

Janice's father was a busy physician and her mother was a practicing attorney. As they told me about Janice's problems, it became clear that they constantly lectured Janice on the importance of academic achievement but they were really uninvolved with the school. In counseling them, I suggested that they take some time from their busy schedules to demonstrate by deed – and not just word – their interest in Janice's academic career. After our talk, Janice's father, in fact, took some time one day during open-school week to visit the class. As he entered the classroom and sat in for a while on a lesson in history, Janice's eyes opened wide with pleasure. A few weeks later, Janice's mother, answering the teacher's call for chaperones, accompanied the class on their trip to the Museum of Natural History. I don't think that it was mere coincidence that following those events, Janice began to show marked improvement in her academic work.

2) Have Realistic Expectations

Living in a free society is a blessing and a curse! On one hand it is great that anyone can become a doctor, a lawyer, a business tycoon or even the president of the United States. On the other hand, if you aren't well on the road to becoming a doctor, a lawyer, a business tycoon or president of the United States, you might feel that you are defective in some way. If you're not in the top reading group in class, it must be your fault. If you don't get 2000 on the SATs, you must be lazy. If you have difficulty with dividing fractions, you must be stupid.

It's no wonder that so many parents, with the best of intentions, push their kids way beyond their potential and capacity. The harsh truth of the matter is that every child is a unique combination of assets and limitations.

Some parents, in an effort to make their child the sharpest pencil in the box, cut and carve too much. By doing so, they can wind up with a dwarfed stub!

One boy, for example, was the child of ambitious, well-educated professional parents. They became alarmed when, in the fourth grade, he began to receive some B grades. "Nothing less than a B+ will do here!" proclaimed the father. "I'm doing my best!" his son said. Arguments ensued and the boy's study time was increased. His after-school activities were curtailed and battles erupted about school and grades and punishments that lasted many years. When the boy went to high school, he rewarded his parents by getting straight "Fs." Finally, they brought him for counseling. When I tested him, I found out that he was a boy who possessed rather average intellectual ability. He did possess rather remarkable "people skills." Fighting a difficult battle with his parents, he developed the all-too-common self-defeating strategy of winning by losing. Had his parents been able to set realistic standards this academic tragedy could have been averted.

Other parents, eager not to impose their desires for academic success, hesitate to impart realistic expectations for achievement. Children who grow up in overly permissive homes may never learn to work up to anywhere near their potential. In a *laissez faire* atmosphere when any old piece of work will do, children can become bored and stunted.

Many studies show that people learn best in a state called "range-of-challenge." Range-of-challenge refers to that level of difficulty and challenge where success seems possible but not too easily achieved.

It's not always easy for a parent to find the range-of-challenge that represents reasonable expectation, but when it is found, achievement usually prevails.

3) Establish A Regular Schedule

Almost all healthy kids need and thrive on routines. If you notice, even young children become comforted if you read the same bedtime story after the shower and after the cookies and milk. The famous psychologist, William James, once wrote that, "Habit is the flywheel that drives our lives."

In my work with youngsters who are having problems in school, I often notice that they come from families where there is very little routine and no strong sense of predictability. In such an atmosphere, it's hard to sit down to do homework or to study for an upcoming test.

One fourth-grader I saw, for example, was having a terrible time in school. Homework assignments were missed, book reports were late and he was frequently tardy. When he did get to school, he often was tired and appeared to be daydreaming.

When I tested the youngster, I was surprised to see how bright he was. In spite of his intelligence, he had little sense of organization. As I got to know this family better, the roots of his problem became more transparent.

His parents were delightful, creative, spontaneous people. In the name of spontaneity, they eschewed schedules or routines. Sometimes, for example, the children, after school, on the spur of the moment, would be whisked down to the shore to have a lobster dinner and would return home at 11 p.m. Meal times were never at a set hour and varied from night to night depending upon what time dad came home from his consulting business.

In the morning, the parents would sometimes get up with the kids but at other times, they were instructed to eat a bowl of cereal and then walk to the bus stop.

After some counseling, these parents were able to establish a better sense of routine for school days and after a short period of time, some of the academic problems began to improve.

A good routine for children during school days involves a regular bedtime and a regular time to wake. It's helpful to have a routine for showers, brushing teeth, story reading, television and of course, time for homework. Homework time, in my experience, is best set late in the afternoon (after some play time) or early in the evening (right after supper).

Even if there isn't assigned homework, the youngster should

be encouraged to use the time set aside for homework to read, study or to work on a project. During homework time, there should be no phone calls, television or going "on-line" and reading the E-mail of the day, or using electronic devices.

The schedule that is established has to be tailored to your own individual family circumstances. The important thing to remember is to adhere to your schedule in a consistent manner. Try it!! You'll see how much easier it becomes for everyone.

4) Reward Desired Behavior

Do you know that the *sine quo* non of learning is reward? Indeed, many psychologists question if, in the absence of reward, any chance of learning can occur at all. From the lowest earthworm to the most brilliant scientist, almost nothing is learned without the "pay-off" of a reward.

Rewards, in order to be effective, do not have to be large. The simple word "great" coming after a desired behavior can be very helpful in reinforcing that behavior and is likely to increase the possibility that the behavior will be repeated.

Rewards can be classified into either "intrinsic" or "extrinsic" categories. "Intrinsic" rewards are those rewards that are attached to the successful completion of an activity.

If a child is beginning to read, for example, there are many intrinsic rewards in learning how to finish a chapter. There's a sense of mastery, an ability to tell yourself a story and satisfy curiosity.

Extrinsic rewards, on the other hand, could be stars on a chart, a bag of M&Ms or a visit to the library.

In general, it is best if kids learn to work for the intrinsic rewards, but often it is necessary, in attempting to teach a desired behavior, to attach an extrinsic reward to the behavior in order to "prime the pump."

Some parents that I have worked with deeply resent having to

SEVEN WAYS TO HELP YOUR CHILD IN SCHOOL

attach an extrinsic reward to an activity. They will say "I don't want to bribe my child into completing his homework, he should do it because he has to do it." In these cases, I often have to patiently explain that reward is not a bribe and that without rewards, little learning will – or can – take place.

If you are, for example, trying to have your child learn to complete his/her homework assignments, the intrinsic reward of eventually getting a good grade may not be enough. You might want to "sweeten" the deal for a while by adding an extrinsic reward. You might, for example, start a chart in the child's room and strike up a contract. Each time the child successfully completes their homework you might place a star on the chart. When there are five stars consecutively earned, you might then give some small reward – a small toy, a candy bar, or some stickers will often be enough do the job.

Once the child establishes the habit of completing assigned homework, it's often no longer necessary to attach extrinsic rewards to the behavior because he/she is now getting the reward of good grades and positive feedback from the school that will reinforce his/her sense of self-esteem.

5) Lower the Level Of Tension in the House

A large number of kids are simply not achieving in school because they are too tense and anxious. A high level of anxiety can markedly interfere with our ability to learn and concentrate.

Have you, for example, ever had the experience of sitting in a doctor's office when he is giving you some instructions about your forthcoming surgery? The chances are that you will leave that office hardly remembering a thing that was said.

Can you imagine what it would be like to be a child sitting in your room upstairs – while your parents are screaming at each other downstairs about their impending divorce? In this all-too-common situation, it's hard to remember if George Washington was the first president of the United States or the new matrimonial attorney.

The famous psychologist Carl Jung once described children as growing creatures who "swim about in the psychic soup of their parents' relationship." Today, almost every family therapist knows that if the parental relationship is strong and parents deal with and own up to their problems, the "psychic soup" of the family is nourishing and nurturing and the growing child can find enough emotional "food" to grow into a healthy and reasonably happy adult. If the "psychic soup" is contaminated by unresolved problems, conflicts and emotional pathology, the resulting emotional contamination can become toxic.

So you want to help your child do well in school? If you do, a good first step would be to resolve some of your own issues and to have the courage to confront and deal with those problems that cause tension. Are there problems with excessive worry, overspending, alcohol, depression? Take steps to help yourself and, by doing so, you might be surprised how helpful this could be for the kids.

6) Ask For Frequent Feedback

One of the problems that I find in our busy public schools is that, in many cases, the only feedback parents get about a child's performance is when report cards arrive – sometimes only three or four times a year.

In such a situation it is hard for parents to know how the child is doing on a week-to-week basis. Is all the homework completed? Is the work sloppy? Are there outstanding assignments?

Many children are not exactly reliable informants when it comes to reporting their progress. Without sufficient feedback from the school, it is hard for even the best of parents to know what to do. One first-aid measure that many psychologists and guidance counselors use, if there is an academic problem, is a weekly report card.

One boy, a freshman in high school, seemed to become overly involved in social activities, parties and clubs. He did very poorly for two marking periods. When his parents asked him whether he had turned in all his assignments, he always responded in the affirmative. Angry arguments and ugly mutual accusations ensued.

When I saw the family together, we developed a contract that included a weekly report card. The parents developed a simple form that listed all the boy's teachers and the statement "Mike has turned in all of his required homework for this week," and a place for each subject and a box for each teacher to check "yes" or "no" and space for the teacher's signature.

The contract was signed in a conference with Mike and his teachers and instructions that Mike would give this form to each teacher on Fridays.

The contract also stated that during the week, Mike's parents would not "bug him" or even remind him of homework. Every Friday, Mike needed to present his signed report. If all homework was turned in, this report acted as Mike's "ticket" to a social weekend. If, however, he failed to keep his end of the bargain, Mike was grounded on Saturday.

After several weeks of "testing" and attempts at manipulation during which his parents remained calm yet firm, Mike got the message and began to learn to rearrange his priorities in a more mature manner.

Without this weekly feedback, Mike still might be floundering. Most teachers that I know will be happy to establish good communication links between school and home.

7) Model a Love For Learning and Discipline

In most family situations, kids grow up not doing what you

tell them to do. Most of the time they do what you do when they get older. Psychologists now say that babies come into the world pre-wired to imitate adult behavior. Studies show that by 8 - 10 weeks of age, or even earlier, healthy infants begin to model their mother's expressions. If for example she smiles, you can see some faint smile lines on the infant's face as he carefully, scans his mother's face for cues. If she frowns, you can see the baby's brow begin to furrow.

As the infant grows into a child, you can observe how much of the child's behavior resembles that of the parent. Do you explode when you are angry? So will he. Do you tend to be shy and uncertain in new situations? So will she. And, so it is with many situations, particularly when it comes to attitudes about learning, teachers, authority and school.

Studies have shown that most children who are avid readers come from houses where reading is seen as a valued activity. The image of watching a parent you love becoming engrossed in an interesting historical novel is not easily lost and, once engraved within the growing child's memory system, may become the prototype for a love of reading and an appreciation of books.

Respect for learning can be encouraged in many other ways as well. Trips to the museum, a nature walk in the woods or starting a stamp collection can all be small sparks that can fire a desire to know more about this wonderful and strange world we live in.

Hours spent watching Sunday afternoon and "Monday Night Football" need to be interspersed with some other curiosity inspiring activities. If not, it is quite predictable that when your child is a sophomore in high school you will begin to complain about his excessive TV watching and his lack of motivation to complete his homework.

Also important are the attitudes that are expressed at home towards school and teachers. In many affluent and sophisticated communities, it is often fashionable to view teachers with a certain amount of subtle – and sometimes not-so-subtle-disdain. You know the kind of remarks: "Those who can do. Those who can't teach." Other parents, educated and competent in their own areas of expertise, feel that they know more about how to teach Spanish or geometry than the teachers. Some parents, resenting their own unhappy experiences in school, are only too ready to find fault with their child's teachers and school.

These negative attitudes by parents towards teachers and school are quickly absorbed by the growing youngsters and, unconsciously, the message is received is that "I don't have to listen to or cooperate with these people."

When parents support and respect their child's teachers and school, the stage is set for a happy and profitable school experience. Are you concerned about your child's upcoming school year? Good! Try applying these seven tips and I suspect that you will be pleasantly surprised at how pleasant (and peaceful) the new school year can be!!

PART FOUR

Petty Dysfunctions

CHAPTER 12

Warning:
Labels Can Be Hazardous to Your Health

Joe is obese. When he was a child, his mother would call him fat every time he gained a pound or two.

Bob refuses possible promotions just when success seems likely. Note: When he was a child, he did poorly in school for two years; his father named him a failure.

"Jim is our athlete; Michael is our student, but Alan is the best mechanic of all the boys."

"Alice is a good kid but she's not the academic type. She will be able to charm people, but she's not going to go to Harvard."

Whether pejorative or complimentary, clinical observation and research have demonstrated that labels can be harmful to psychological development and growth.

In my work as a psychologist, I am impressed by the capacity of a child to be shaped by the expectations communicated through labels and names that surround them. Contrary to the old childhood adage that "sticks and stones can break my bones but names can never harm me," names can and DO cause emotional damage in various ways. Let's explore some of them.

1) A Label Can Become A Self-Fulfilling Prophecy

Some months ago, I was consulted by a young attorney and his wife. They were concerned about their eight-year-old son's inability to relate well to other children. As they spoke about their son, it became clear that the boy had many problems relating to other youngsters. He could not share or cooperate and when his friends did not do his bidding, he lashed out in an aggressive, competitive, angry manner. While a few of his classmates seemed to be in awe of his hostile behavior, most resented his overly-aggressive responses.

The "nickname" that his parents gave him when he was young? Tiger! "Tiger's" parents began to boast about his physical prowess when he was still an infant and they exaggerated and were pleased by his strength compared to other nursery school children. Unaware of his own motivation, "Tiger's" dad subtly encouraged his son to become a bully who was allowed to traumatize the neighborhood.

Psychologist Dr. Robert Rosenthal, in one famous experiment, demonstrated the capacity of a prophecy to become self-fulfilled. Working with teachers prior to the opening of school, he identified certain children as "academic spurters" who were likely to achieve. In reality, he chose the pupils at random. They had previously shown no greater intellectual promise than the rest of the group.

Amazingly, those children who were labeled as having good intellectual potential fulfilled the prophecy. At the end of the year, when all the children were tested, they showed more incidence of intellectual gain and achievement.

In a similar experiment with children in a day camp, it was found that kids were more likely to learn to swim when their waterfront counselors were advised that they were "ready."

2) Labels are Not Always Correct

A child may be misclassified on the basis of a single psychological test or by an all-too-brief observation by an inexperienced or overly confident teacher. Well trained psychologists know that psychological diagnoses or educational labels should only be applied after repeated observation and testing.

Several years ago, I tested a child who was regarded as being "slow" by his parents. During the initial interview, the child's parents (both of whom had advanced graduate degrees) kept comparing his rather poor intellectual achievement to the academic attempts of his two older sisters. At one point, the father said, "Well, I guess every child can't be a genius. We love him, even though he's a bit backward."

Careful intellectual testing of the boy revealed that his intelligence exceeded fully 87 percent of the population. In this family of intellectual giants, he was indeed the pygmy but in objective comparison to the general population, he was quite adequate. Because he had been cast in the role of the "slow" child in the family, he had "given up" in school and increasingly began to seek self-esteem in non academic areas.

Had Helen Keller's mother accepted the dim prognosis for her daughter, the world would never have been enriched by her many contributions. In spite of having been told by doctors that her childhood illnesses would leave her retarded, the family hired tutors to work with her in every way possible. Many years later, Helen Keller graduated *cum laude* from Radcliffe College.

3) A Label Can Create Fear

In many primitive cultures if people thought themselves to be bewitched or cursed they would literally become sick. If the curse was not removed, they would often die. Voodoo, if you believe in its power, can kill with fear. Dr. Jerome Frank, a noted psychologist described many cases of people who were destroyed by fear or who were restored to health by hope. Although there are, fortunately, few people in contemporary society who believe in witchcraft, there are many whose lives are haunted by a fearful label given to them when they were children.

Lisa is a painfully tortured young woman who worries constantly about her health. When she has a brief bout of indigestion, she is sure she has cancer. If she has a headache, she fears a brain tumor. As a child, Lisa was doted upon by an anxious mother who often told Lisa when her minor allergies would act up that she needed to take good care of herself because she had a tendency to be *sickly* and that she was *fragile*.

4) Labels Mean Different Things to Different People

Psychologists know that most communication is based on words. The meaning of words are always based on our previous experiences. Words, in the last analysis often mean very different things to different people.

Susan's mother, for example, views a person as being obese if she's a few pounds overweight. "You're *fat*," she would yell at Susan if she gained a pound or two. Now that Susan is 40 years old, she is objectively quite thin. She wears a size six dress and when she gained three pounds recently, she went with a friend to an overeater anonymous meeting. The other women in the group were amazed by Susan and one of them said, "Honey, you don't know what *fat* is all about."

In some homes, being a *good* child means staying out of jail. In other homes, being *good* is a euphemism for immediate and explicit obedience to mother.

5) Labels Limit Freedom and Opportunity to Grow

Overly zealous labeling can cripple a person's capacity to develop talents and abilities that aren't consistent with the label. For a long time in our society, fortunately somewhat less so now, certain behaviors were rigorously labeled as "masculine" or "feminine." Because of the fear of being a "tomboy," many a young girl has learned to appear frightened and to squeal with appropriate "feminine" hysteria when she sees a mouse or a spider. More serious is the situation of the multitudes of women who hid the light of their abilities under the bushel of sex-role prejudices lest men reject them.

Abbie was a highly competent woman who was offered a substantial job. She refused the position, but soon found herself depressed and irritable. "I would love the job," she told me, "but I just couldn't put myself in the position of making so much more money than Frank. I'm not sure our marriage could withstand it."

As a practicing psychologist, I am often astounded by women who still come to regard their own success as a liability rather than an asset. Although all of the research evidence is still not in, there is the strong suggestion that many women's "math-phobia" is related to adolescent fears of being too interested in "boy-stuff."

Men, too, can be restricted by labeling. The man who feels that he always has to be "tough" can have great difficulty expressing his more tender feelings, while the man who always has to be the "nice guy" can run into industrial-strength problems when he needs to fire an irresponsible employee.

In view of awesome power of labels and names to influence behavior, it becomes vitally important to know what can be done to protect both yourself and your children from the dangers. Here are a few suggestions that can help you use the power of labels wisely.

1) Resist Your Own urge to Classify

Most of us feel more comfortable when the people around us fit into predictable little roles. Out of this need to live in an orderly universe, many parents are just too eager to classify behavior. Even when the labels are positive, too many evaluative comments may cause a child to stake out a premature claim to a particular area of competency. Allowed to wait longer, the boundaries might become larger.

Family therapists know that consciously or unconsciously, children get cast into certain roles in the drama of family. Sometimes they get placed in a particular role as a result of a brief audition. Acceptance of the fact that much in life is uncertain can help a parent to avoid the illusion of certainty that labeling brings and can allow one to live more comfortably with life's necessary ambiguity.

2) Remember, Behavior Changes

Some undesirable childhood behavior is virtually characteristic of particular ages.

It is common psychological knowledge, for example, that some stealing is usual in a child of six or seven. At this age, the child is beginning to learn about the concept of private property and the taking of toys or objects that belong to another may represent no more than a form of experimentation in ownership. If the behavior is permitted to continue without reprimand, a child is likely to continue to steal. Curiously, if too much is made of an incident or two, overzealous attempts to suppress the behavior may only serve to reinforce. In a moment of anger and fear, a parent may say things that they will later regret. Calling Billy a "thief" because he returns home with a toy that doesn't belong to him can boomerang. If Billy comes to see himself as a "thief," his future actions will only serve to confirm his self-image. A strong statement such as "Billy, you are not *allowed* to take things that don't belong to you" can teach without destroying the pupil.

During adolescence, we know that a certain amount of rebelliousness and "testing the limits" are par for the course. It is easy during such times, for parents to lose their sense of humor and patience. One patient I saw, for example, had great problems relating to authority. He often would perceive his bosses as picking on him and had difficulty following directions. Although he was an extremely gifted salesman, his attitude with his superiors constantly got him into trouble. He could be friendly and cooperative with his customers but whenever his boss would ask him to fill out an expense form more carefully, he would sulk or display his annoyance in obvious ways. He lost several jobs because of the massive chip he wore on his shoulder.

When he was a teenager and had begun to test the limit of authority, his angry and punitive father often would say, "You're a *born rebel.*" Said and heard often enough, the name became the game.

3) Keep the Standards Reasonable

There can be no question that we live in a most exciting and stimulating society. All kinds of opportunities are possible and never before in the history of mankind has the success or failure of a person's life depended so much on our own resources and merit. The opportunities of such an open society are not an unmixed blessing.

In our dreams of success for our children, we often keep "upping the ante" until there is a breaking point. We sometimes push our kids beyond their naturally endowed limits and then *we* or *they* come to view them as a *failure.*

One family I know had a daughter who showed a considerable amount of singing and acting ability. By the time she was in fourth grade, she had the lead role in the Thanksgiving play. After hundreds of dancing, singing and acting lessons, she became the star of her high school play. In college, as a drama major, she once again had top billing. After graduation from college, she was now confronted by the harsh reality of trying to break into the professional world of theater. Working as a waitress at night, she would spend her days going to auditions. Often, if a part was advertised, there were as many as 50 to 100 aspiring applicants. After the better part of a year, her family became increasingly impatient with her and they began to criticize her efforts and her approach to getting a job. The criticism led to arguing and the arguing led to fighting and the fighting led to name calling. In the midst of a bitter argument, her enraged mother yelled, "Let's face it – you're a *failure.*"

Shortly after this argument, the young woman became severely depressed and no longer went to auditions. She came to label herself as a "failure." Totally forgotten during this frustrating period of time by the young woman as well as her family was the harsh reality of the fact that New York City has thousands of gifted, aspiring, talented young actresses – all of whom are waiting for "a chance." There simply are not enough jobs available for the multitude of gifted and talented actresses.

This young woman certainly was not a *failure.* She was indeed talented and gifted. The odds were simply not in her favor.

4) If You Need to use a Label — At Least Make It a Positive One

It is best not to use or abuse labels at all. If you MUST label, at least keep your labels positive.

When the label is a positive one, you are opening the door to positive future change and better behavior. Let us imagine that Mike, your 16-year-old son, is left in charge of the house while the rest of the family has to go to Boston overnight. Continuing the plot, imagine now that you tell Mike that he can have *one,* and only *one,* friend stay with him overnight. Mike agrees. Now further imagine (its not hard to do) that you return home to find evidence that a big party took place. In trying to corroborate your suspicion, you speak to your next door neighbor who tells you that there were at least 50 kids in the backyard making noise and the party did not break up until neighbors complained about the noise to police. Armed with this information, you confront Mike about the party. Mike replies, "There wasn't a big party at all, there were just two other people that came over. They just dropped over." What to do? What to say to Mike?

MULTIPLE CHOICE ANSWERS (CHOOSE THE BEST)
A. "You're a *liar.*"
B. "You're *lying* again."
C. "I'm sick and tired of your bold-faced *lies.*"
D. "Listen, Mike, you're basically a *good* kid. *Lying* about the party may make you feel good for the moment, but since you're an *honest* guy, why don't you just tell me the truth?"

There is no 100 percent guarantee in any action, but as a practicing psychotherapist, I think you're clearly improving your chances of getting Mike to stop lying if you choose option "D."

In dealing with your kids, learn to condemn the *act* and not the *person.* A rotten deed is something a child can change; being a *rotten* person is much more permanent and conveys the message that change is not possible.

When in doubt, it is always wiser to trust your child's ability to change and to emerge successfully on the other side of an undesirable patch of behavior.

5) Don't Let an Old Label Stunt Your Own – and Then Your Child's Growth

In order to truly understand and help your children, you had best start with yourself. If you don't understand the old labels that direct your behavior, you are contagious! Your child might very well catch those same harmful labels from you.

Do you see yourself as *ugly?* If you do, you are going to be overly concerned about your child's appearance. Do you see yourself as *unpopular?* If so, it will be hard for you to refrain from interference in your child's social life. Do you have a family myth that has been passed on to you? Is it a myth that contains dangerous or negative psychological labels? Often, I am surprised by the number of people who are not consciously aware of the names that they call themselves.

In dealing with our kids, we have to watch out for a curious psychological mechanism called *projection.* When we use projection, we tend to disown unfavorable traits in ourselves and attribute them to someone else. If we are *stingy* and refuse to confront, acknowledge and own up to our own stinginess, we may wind up accusing others of being tight with the purse strings.

If you look carefully, you will notice that most of the time, you are annoyed with another person's trait. It is often that same trait that you have been wrestling with within your own personality.

One mother, for example, was extremely self-indulgent. All of her friends know how little she would ever do for others. This woman had some vague perception of the extent of her self-absorption and, in the past, some of her friends had spoken to her in annoyance. Not really owning up to the trait, she projected it onto her teenage daughter and constantly called her *selfish.* During one family session, the daughter (in many ways a healthy teenager) complained, "I don't get it – the minute I don't do exactly what she wants, she calls me *selfish.* Does she have a problem or what?"

So before you start giving unfavorable labels to others, you would do better to carefully examine yourself in order to better understand why you are so annoyed.

Surely, the "sticks and stones" of psychological names may not "break our bones" – but they sure can hurt. Are you using labels in a healthy, rather than a destructive manner?

CHAPTER 13

Doer's Block:
Procrastination Isn't Lazy

"**I** *don't know why I do it: I wait until the very last minute. Then, it's a gigantic rush until I get it finished!*"

"*My desk is piled so high with stuff that I feel I'll never get to it. When I get that feeling, I just sit and stare at it or I go out and have some more coffee. When I get back, the pile looks even higher!*"

"*I promised myself that I would work on the project that has to be in by the end of this month for an hour and a half every night. For the past ten days, I must have chewed up a dozen pencils. I daydream and can't seem to focus on what I need to do.*"

All of the above complaints – and many others like them – were made to me by patients during the past several months. The people, themselves, were different: Some were young and others were old. Some were well established and others were just beginning their careers. Although different in many ways, they all shared a common problem: All were procrastinators!

During the past several years, the number of people who complain about procrastination seems to be increasing. More and more people feel pushed and pulled in different directions.

People who are procrastinators are often dismissed by others, as well as themselves, as simply being lazy. In my experience, calling others or yourself lazy is a very lazy, simplistic explanation for what can often be a fairly complex problem.

As a result of our increasing preoccupation with procrastination, psychologists have begun to take a long, hard objective look at this all-too-common problem. While the full mystery of procrastination still needs to be solved, here are some of the reasons and motives that seem to underlie chronic problems of procrastination:

1) Getting Back

As strange as it may seem, many bouts of procrastination represent an unconscious form of getting back at "authority" when we perceive ourselves as being treated unfairly. A brief case history:

Mr. Frank (fictitious name), age 43, came to see me because he was afraid that he would lose his job because of continuous procrastination. Mr. Frank was the vice president of a small but successful company. For the first five years on this job, he worked efficiently and well. Each year, he received a handsome bonus and a promotion as well. His difficulty with procrastination began about a year before he came to see me, following a reorganization of the company's profit-sharing plan. Mr. Frank felt he was not treated as well as he should have been and complained to his boss, a rather overbearing, somewhat "bottom-line" type. His complaint was handled by the boss telling him that, "There is nothing I can do. This is the plan that the chief financial officer has suggested – and we need to live with it." Shortly after this, the problems with procrastination began. It wasn't until the patient had a vivid dream one night of "being out on a picket line outside a factory" that he began to realize he was truly on a "slow-down strike."

Raised by a harsh, sometimes abusive immigrant father, this man, as a youngster, had few effective means of "getting back" at his dad until he hit upon the frustrating tactic of delay. Confronted with frustration in his adult life, he reverted back to a child-like way of "getting back."

2) It Can't be Perfect

Often, underlying a pattern of "putting it off" is the lurking fear that the task won't be completed perfectly. Procrastinators are often thinly disguised perfectionists.

In my work with graduate students, I often find that some of my brightest students spend painful hours before their word-processors hesitating to type in even one word. Sometimes, in their distress, they come to me complaining "I can't get started." They often are shocked when I suggest to them that they write any old thing down. Just let the ideas flow freely. Forget about grammar, spelling and repetition. I remind them that they can always do a second draft and that it is easier to edit something than to produce it. Often this strategy can be helpful.

3) I'll be Happy

Many studies have demonstrated that when we complete a task, we often feel a sense of gratification from the release of tension that this completion brings. Can you recall, for example, the slight reduction in tension that you experienced when you completed your income tax form, licked the envelope and finally deposited the darn thing in the mail box? Can you remember the small relief that you felt when, after putting it off for months, you finally made an appointment with your dentist and had that pesky filling replaced? I bet you can think of your own examples in which finishing a task or a chore brings a sense of relief and pleasure.

Strange as it may seem, many people, in spite of their consciously stated desire to be happy, often behave in a manner that will punish themselves. These people often shoot themselves in the foot – sometimes in subtle ways. Procrastination, in many cases, may be the bullet that is used to create a sense of discomfort.

4) Making a Little Excitement

Many of the best movies around are called "cliff-hangers." In a typical cliff-hanger movie, the excitement builds and builds. Will the cops solve the mystery of where the kidnapping victim has been taken before she is murdered? Will the doctors on "E.R." get a new heart to Chicago from Los Angeles in time to save a life? Will the FBI find the terrorist bomb that is planted under the theme park in Disneyworld before the explosion takes place? WOW! What a relief when the kidnapping victim is found, the new heart gets to Chicago, and the terrorist bomb under Disneyworld is defused – all in the nick of time!!

The theme of things being done at the last moment – in the last few seconds before midnight – is an old drama in our cultural experiences. It is no wonder that some people, finding their lives boring and routine, create a sense of dramatic excitement by leaving things to the last moment and then, with a great deal of flurry and rush, finally cross the finish line. Once over the finish line, there's a sense of triumph and some restoration of pride "I did it – I finally did it!" It's not the New York Marathon, it's just a routine out-of-pocket expense report that needed to be turned in to the boss – but it's finished at last!

5) Have Fun Now – Pay Later – Maybe!

If you ask a typical five year old, "Would you rather have 10 cents now or $10 tomorrow?" Their response is usually, "I'll take the 10 cents now."

When you pose the same question of a reasonably intelligent and well adjusted eight-year-old, the response is likely to be, "Are you kidding? Of course I'll wait until tomorrow!"

For many people in our pleasure-oriented society, the difference between short-term and long-term pleasure has never been learned. Not having learned this fundamental lesson of maturity can lead to a series of minor and sometimes major disasters. The immediate pleasure of buying by using a credit card unwisely can lead to personal bankruptcy. The immediate pleasures of drinking a great deal on Saturday night can lead to the Sunday hangover.

Sometimes, the chronic procrastinator, not knowing the difference between short-term and long-term pleasure, will watch the exciting TV program but never get to the homework and so, unpleasant tasks pile up. Instead of paying the piper a small sum now, the interest piles up and in the future the debt becomes quite large.

If you have a problem with procrastination, think long and hard about some of these things – and see which one (or two) of them apply to you. Meanwhile, even if you haven't figured out exactly what underlies your own procrastination profile, *here are some practical tips to pursue:*

1) Break It Down to Manageable Proportions

If you would tell a newlywed bride at the age of 25 that she will have to wash two to three million coffee cups in her lifetime, the chances are that she would never get started. (She might even panic so much that she could cancel the wedding!) Paralyzed by procrastination, she might never even get near the sink!

When an unpleasant task looms ahead, try to break it down to manageable proportions. When you do, it no longer seems so impossible. On a personal note: When I was finishing up my graduate work at Columbia University, I was confronted with having to write my thesis for my Ph.D. I had already completed my research but for days and weeks, the idea of writing *a* "thesis" seemed to be a monumental, impossible task. Often, I would sit at my desk and worry about how I would ever accomplish this task. One day, worried about my procrastination and inability to get into the project, I spoke to a friend of mine who had completed his dissertation a few years before. He told me that he had had a similar problem with getting started but finally solved his problem by thinking about the task – not as a thesis but as six long term papers.

He said to me, "You have done many term papers in the past. Just get to one chapter at a time." His advice worked like magic and, after working on my first "chapter," I took a brief break and then worked on the second one. Within a couple of months, the "impossible" task was completed. Since that time, I have passed on his wise advice to many graduate students.

2) Reward Yourself For a Task Well Done

Let's pretend it's a typical Saturday afternoon. There are some things that you need to do that are not particularly pleasant. You might, for example, have to deliver a load of clothes to the dry cleaners, wash the kitchen floor and give the dog a bath. There are also some things that you would like to do on that Saturday. You might want to finish the last 50 pages of the novel that you are enjoying. You might also be looking forward to calling your old friend in Los Angeles. You might even be longing to spend a half hour or so resting in the new hammock that has never been used.

All too often, people with procrastination problems read the book, call their friend in Los Angeles and rest in the hammock. This approach is a sure recipe for cooking up a pot of procrastination. One little trick that can help break a chronic pattern of procrastination is to do the unpleasant task first, and as a reward, get to the things that we want to do.

This technique of rewarding yourself after an unpleasant task is called the Premack Principle by psychologists (named after the psychologist who helped many break the habit of procrastination). In the hypothetical example given, it would be wise for the person to deliver the load of clothes to the dry cleaner with the clear understanding that when returning home, he/she will then call the friend in Los Angeles. After washing the kitchen floor, the internal contract will stipulate finishing the last 50 pages of the novel. Finally, after the dog has been bathed and dried, it's time for the hammock.

3) Do!! Don't Stew!

Many times, the procrastination machine is fueled by a painful mix of 50 percent fear, 25 percent worry and 25 percent anxiety. Each procrastinator of this type has their own favorite blend.

Often, something is put off because the procrastinator simply fears the results. Like an ostrich, they put their heads in the sand when confronted with an anxiety-provoking situation. Like ostriches, this technique is likely to provide momentary relief but the long-term result places you in more danger.

One patient of mine, for example, developed a chronic cough. Her father had died of lung cancer many years ago and she was also a fairly heavy smoker.

For months, she agonized about going to the doctor. She was sure she had lung cancer and that nothing could be done to help her. At times, she would promise herself to call her physician for an X-ray; paralyzed by fear-fueled procrastination, she would put it off. She began to lose sleep because of her worries and obsessed for hours about her possibilities of having lung cancer.

Finally, after much work, I finally convinced her to call her physician. I explained to her that there were only two possibilities.

She either had lung cancer or she did not have lung cancer. If she didn't have lung cancer, she would be relieved to know it. If she did, indeed, have lung cancer, the sooner that she started treatment, the better chance she would have for survival. This simple logic, however, took a long time to sink in.

When she finally broke through her barrier of fear, she contacted her physician and was greatly relieved to learn that she had no evidence of cancer. Her chronic bronchitis and allergy yielded to appropriate treatment within two weeks. Afterwards, she said, "Was I foolish or what? I could have spared myself many sleepless nights if I just did it sooner."

4) Don't Bite Off More Than You Can Chew

Remember when you were young and your mother told you never to bite off more than you could chew? Well, she was right! All too many procrastinators are simply overloaded with activity. This overbooking of activity eventually causes many problems. Like a juggler who successfully juggles twelve balls and then adds three more, the overloaded person is likely to drop a few from time to time. One man I know, for example, was a classic "people pleaser." He simply could never say "no." In addition to a stressful professional career, he added to his burden by becoming over-involved in outside activities. When his daughter's team needed a softball coach, he volunteered. He did such a great job that the following year they asked him to run the entire softball program in town. He was so successful at that activity that the minister of his church asked him to head up the fundraising campaign for a new social hall. That position soon led into a campaign for the school board.

Overwhelmed by his many activities and never allowing any spare time to attend to his own needs, he soon became exhausted and burnt out. While in this state, he put almost everything off and began to procrastinate even the simplest of tasks.

Like the famous "Peter Principle," this man's high level of

dedication and competence lead to increasing responsibility and harder tasks. Exhausted, he eventually reached an unhappy level of incompetence.

When he finally learned to politely say "no," he began to shed some load and, as a result, was able to handle his life without being plagued by procrastination.

5) Remember! Perfection is For the Gods – Not You!!

Our society, in many ways, is becoming tougher and more competitive. As we move into a world economy, most jobs have become rougher. Many large companies have maintained their profits by "downsizing." As a result of this progressive cutting away of fat, the workers who are left have to work longer, harder and standards begin going up, as rewards often get leaner.

Our kids are feeling the pressure to become perfect as well. SAT courses have given way to pre-SAT courses which now are giving way to individual tutoring before you take a pre-SAT test. There's a vague sense that if you don't get a near perfect score, you'll never get into a decent college or decent job.

Even television, by exposing us to "perfect" performances, can make us doubt our own ability and cause us to procrastinate.

One girl I knew used to enjoy ice skating and would have many pleasant afternoons with her friends skating indoors as well as outdoors. After the last Olympics, she had decided to give up skating. When I asked her why, she sadly said, "I could never skate the way that those athletes do. I feel like an elephant trying to dance the ballet." How sad, that she gave up an activity that could have brought her pleasure!

The next time you procrastinate, ask yourself, "Am I afraid this won't be good enough? Is that what is making me put things off?"

If, deep down in your heart you know that the answer is yes, remember that perfectionism produces procrastination. It's okay to be imperfect; it's not okay to *GIVE UP!* Good Luck!

CHAPTER 14

Guilt:
Take in Moderation

*P*hil V., age 47, finally gets the promotion that he has always wanted. Strangely, he finds himself sleepless and unhappy.

Cynthia R., age 17, has had her first sexual experience. Shortly afterwards, her grades slipped badly and she was in danger of not graduating.

Arthur S., age 23, robs a drugstore and brutally assaults the pharmacist. With some of the stolen money, he buys a new tape deck and some clothes. He feels no sense of wrongdoing.

These three people share a common problem. Whether conscious or unconscious, excessive or insufficient, the problem is *GUILT.*

Never before has the question of guilt become so pressing. Americans watched in fascination as the O.J. Simpson and Oklahoma City trials progressed. There seems to be a thread of cynical disregard for morality that runs through the entire fabric of society. High government officials are convicted of conspiracy, students steal examinations, healthcare workers commit insurance fraud, prominent lawyers are convicted of income tax evasion and tobacco company executives lie about their research.

Words like "honesty" or "truth" are regarded as being "square" by those who view themselves as being above morality. Others, oppressed by needless guilt, torture themselves because they do not live up to the most unreasonable expectations.

In recent years, psychologists who have studied the problem of guilt have come to realize that this universal feeling is, indeed, the most powerful triple-edged tool of conscience. Used *properly*, *guilt* can be the gentle guiding force that can steer your life back into proper channels. Used *unwisely*, guilt can cripple your happiness and health. *Ignored guilt* can never nourish your humanity and potential for growth. More than ever, it becomes vital to learn how to make guilt work *for* you rather than *against* you.

If we are healthy, we feel guilt when we have violated some internal rule of conscience. When guilty, many physical changes take place within our bodies. Our rate of breathing changes and we may blush or perspire. Our mouths may feel dry and full of "cotton."

In some primitive tribes, guilt is determined by placing a dry leaf in an accused person's mouth to see if it becomes moistened by saliva. If it remains dry, the accused is assumed to be guilty. Modern lie-detector tests measure subtle physical changes such as perspiration and blood pressure in a more sophisticated manner than a dry leaf.

While we share more primitive feelings such as rage or terror with lower forms of life, the capacity to be guided by conscience makes us uniquely human and opens a channel to higher sources of wisdom. As a boy, George Washington wrote, "Labor to keep alive in your breast that little spark of celestial fire-conscience!"

Many of us, when guilty, feel as if we are carrying a great

weight while others become increasingly irritable, moody and overly defensive. Sometimes, the source of our guilt may be quite *conscious.* We know exactly what we did wrong and feel badly about our actions. All too frequently, the wellsprings of guilt remain *unconscious.* Rooted in the soil of childhood memories and nourished by lack of awareness, the weeds of unconscious can strangle the fruits of happiness and prevent the growth of healthy personality.

One patient I worked with could find little happiness in her life in spite of "having it all." She had a fine and loving husband, great kids, good health, an interesting job and no financial worries. She couldn't understand the discrepancy between her inner unhappiness and her outward success. As she explored her life, she became aware that much of her unhappiness was caused by an oppressive sense of guilt.

As a child, her mother often placed her in charge of a brother who was 10 years younger. She would sometimes be blamed if he got into mischief and she would be accused of "not babysitting him properly."

Spoiled and indulged, the younger brother achieved little, and by the time he was 35, he had become a chronic alcoholic who drifted about and would only contact his older sister when he needed a handout.

Disregarding the fact that she had tried everything possible to help her brother, this woman experienced an enormous amount of unconscious guilt because of her inability to stop his alcoholism and irresponsibility. With the help of therapy and attendance at Al-Anon meetings, she began to understand her sources of unrealistic guilt and was gradually able to experience more happiness in her life.

Each of us seems to have our own special sensitivity to guilt. For some, even a minor transgression of an inner moral code can trigger painful pangs. Others, unhappily, can commit major crimes and not even lose a moment of sleep.

Our own individual guilt responses are determined by a variety of sources. Our early childhood experiences are certainly important. If you were handled too severely and, if this severity was not tempered by considerable love, you are likely to grow up with an excessive burden of guilt. Conversely, a home atmosphere of excessive permissiveness and leniency can prove equally destructive. Recently, for example, I saw a young man whose life was crippled by his constant use of drugs and irresponsible behavior. He was raised by older parents who rarely made any demands upon him for responsibility. As a result of this indulgence, he never learned to defer his impulses nor could he feel normal guilt.

Parental models and peer groups when we are growing up can also determine the extent of our guilt reactions. While it is quite true that "birds of a feather flock together," it is also known that any particular "flock" will exert powerful pressure upon any new "bird" to conform to the group's moral code. A sensitive or an immature individual may prove to be particularly vulnerable to such external pressures.

The capacity to feel guilt is normal and necessary for living in a civilized society. For all too many people, their "guilt buttons" seem to be either too tight or too loose.

Excessive guilt, on one hand or *insufficient* guilt on the other, can result in a lopsided balance between your own needs and the needs of others can result in tragedy.

Excessive guilt can destroy a person's happiness more than any other feeling. When you feel too guilty, you often become your own judge who hands down a harsh sentence of unhappiness and self-torture. Some punish themselves with depression, worry or even excessive work to assuage their need for self-punishment. Profoundly guilty people require a daily "quota of suffering."

Insufficient guilt, on the other hand, can result in a life that is stunted and maimed. Many chronic criminals are unable to feel a normal sense of guilt or shame. Unencumbered by burdens of ethics or by commonly held standards of "fair play," these amoral individuals may ruin their own life as well as the lives of many others in the course of their antisocial and criminal careers. The person who has no capacity to feel guilt is as dangerous as a spark in a firecracker factory!

Because guilt is a problem that we all need to cope with, here are some tips that I, as a practicing psychologist, can offer to you in dealing with the troublesome yet human feeling.

1) Don't Blame the Sun and the Moon and the Stars

"We make guilty of our disasters, the sun, the moon and the stars; as if we were victims by necessity..."

Although these lines were penned by William Shakespeare centuries ago, there are still many people today who would gladly blame *anything* or *anyone* for their own actions.

I am sometimes appalled at the large number of self-indulgent, immature people who grind and pound psychology's increasing knowledge about the effects of unfortunate early experiences into a universal salve to ease troubled consciences. While it is certainly true that many individuals come from terribly troubled families or indeed live in difficult circumstances, a person has *some* degree of choice in almost every situation.

The first step, therefore, in dealing with guilt is to acknowledge and own-up to our own responsibility and shortcomings. In a sense, we need to do some self-exploration and determine our own "guilt-quotient."

Do you blame everything on yourself? Are you too prone to excuse yourself for any action? Once you understand your own reaction to guilt, you are well on the way to appropriate self-control. Most people, when they truly embark on the exciting voyage of self-discovery, find treasures of information about themselves which can be used to purchase greater personal happiness and more adequate self-control. Many of you may find that you are still bound by chains of childhood "shoulds." Although some of these archaic "shoulds" still have a purpose, many of them need to be placed in the same attic as one's old teddy bear. For others, an honest appraisal of your "guilt quotient" will turn up, instead of too many "shoulds" too *few* "shoulds" that often masquerade as a sense of entitlement for injustices that were committed in the past.

One woman, for example, treated those about her with a sense of contempt. She would often expect extraordinary favors from others which she had no intent to return. She rationalized her behavior as being the result of an unhappy childhood that was marked by a considerable amount of rejection by her mother who did not desire another child. As she came to realize that her own abuse did not give her a free ticket to abuse others, she gradually began to take more responsibility for her many failed and unhappy relationships.

2) Share Your Guilt with Someone Else

Like a sharp pebble in your shoe, an unshared feeling of guilt can press against your conscience and cripple your ability to travel a comfortable path through life.

The Judeo-Christian tradition of confession, when used properly, brought comfort and solace to millions, before the advent of modern psychology.

It was modern psychology that recognized how *many* problems are rooted in unshared and unexplored guilt. Almost all psychologists have seen instances where the sharing of guilty feelings and thoughts bring relief from unnecessary and burdensome guilt. Sometimes, confession of guilt to another person can bring almost immediate and dramatic improvement in a person's feelings about themselves and others.

One of the healing qualities of group therapy comes from

open and frank discussion with other human beings about one's own feelings of guilt. In such a safe and confidential atmosphere, a person may begin to learn techniques to manage their guilt.

Sharing guilt with others requires a certain degree of good judgment. Beware of sharing any of these feelings with those who love to gossip or those who are out of touch with their own feelings. You also need to know that, while "openness" in a close relationship can be helpful, I have observed situations where "telling all" becomes a powerful weapon that can be used to punish and torture another person.

If the result of such a "confession" is likely to have more destructive than constructive consequences, it might be kinder and wiser for you to share your guilt with a trained therapist or a trusted religious advisor.

3) Don't Let Others Manipulate You with Unrealistic Guilt

Unfortunately, there are some people who play upon your sympathy and prey upon your guilt. By pushing your guilt button, they attempt to manipulate and control. Often, this kind of manipulation is accompanied by protests that *all* is being done in the name of love. One couple I saw for counseling had quite a problem with the husband's mother, a widow who lived alone. For several years after the death of her husband, both son and daughter-in-law dutifully tended to her every need. She was brought to their home for the holidays and was treated with respect and love. Almost every weekend was spent doing something, at least on one day, for mother. Phone calls were made daily.

Trouble began when the husband and wife planned to spend a week of vacation with friends in Mexico. Initially, upon hearing the news, the mother began to make statements like, "What will happen if I get sick when you are away?" (She was in excellent health.) Her attempts to control became bolder and louder until she finally said, tearfully, "How can you do this to me – I'm your mother – I always took care of you?"

The pushing of her son's "guilt button" almost had the desired effect and he nearly canceled their long-awaited vacation. Fortunately as he began to sort out his feelings, he came to realize that his mother's plea for him to cancel his vacation really arose out of an illegitimate need to control his life. He knew that, in reality, his mother had an excellent support system. He had a brother who lived close by and an aunt who was only a few houses away. With some tribulation, he went on vacation and did have a good time. Curiously enough, so did his mother who spent the week with his brother and friends.

Pushing your guilt button in order to control or manipulate is *all too common*. Some charities, for example, send you all manner of unwanted merchandise; they hope to raise funds by raising your level of guilt. To those who attempt to control you making you feel unrealistically guilty, you need to protect yourself with a healthy dose of your own independence, and perhaps a lesson in decent human relationships.

4) Learn to Love Yourself as Much as Your Neighbor

The ancient "Golden Rule" for human relationships contains an important lesson for those who feel excessive guilt: *Unless you can come to love and respect yourself, it becomes almost impossible for you to love and respect your neighbor.*

Many unhappy and guilty people have two yardsticks. One yardstick is flexible, understanding and kind. This benign, easy going yardstick is used in measuring and judging the behavior of others. The other yardstick is rigid, harsh and unyielding. This one is often used to judge one's own behavior. On a weekly basis, I see many people who, although able to forgive others, relentlessly *persecute themselves.*

Ancient biblical wisdom teaches and modern clinical observation confirms the simple fact that if you can't forgive yourself, you will truly have trouble forgiving others.

Some people in switching yardsticks, save the rigid, harsh, unyielding one for others, while they reserve the flexible, forgiving one for themselves. True measurement consists of using the same yardstick for everyone, including yourself. A rubber yardstick has about as much value as a convoluted conscience.

5) Don't Wallow in Guilt

Engulfed in a swamp of guilt and self-pity, you can never rebuild a life on the solid foundation of self-respect. Sometimes, constantly dwelling on one's guilt becomes an interpersonal technique for avoiding the possible intrusion of others. Blaming yourself frequently and flamboyantly can often be a technique for warding off the blame of others. By *loudly* proclaiming your own guilt, you can force others into *whispering* their genuine grievance.

Recently, for example, I was working with a 17-year-old boy who truly refused to take any responsibility for his life. In spite of being very bright, he was failing in school. He rarely turned in homework assignments and always had an excuse for not having the term papers completed. At home, he spent hours on the internet and when asked to take the garbage out he replied, "No problem, I'll do it in a little while." Needless to say, the garbage remained until, in the service of nasal self defense, his mother or father would undertake the monumental task of throwing the garbage into the outside can.

In a family session, when confronted by his parents with some of his irresponsible behavior, he loudly and tearfully began a session of self-flagellation.

"I'm really terrible," he proclaimed. "They do so much for me, and I don't even take out the garbage. I'm a lazy baby, that's all

I am... I'm just no good."

By the end of the session, his parents were comforting him and offered to lend him money towards a car. It was quite clear to me that this boy had learned an effective technique for manipulation through wallowing in his guilt.

Other people continue to berate themselves with guilt in a quiet, private manner. Relationships that are bound together by the ties of guilt can often bring disaster to all. Guilt that continues indefinitely cannot help anyone nor can it repair any wrong. Just as it is healthy to be able to be restrained by guilt at certain times, it is just as important to be able to knock down an old prison of remorse and use the bricks and mortar of the old to build a road to the future.

6) When You Say "I'm Sorry," DO Something About It:

Sometimes the simplest and most efficient way to deal with guilt is to say "I'm sorry..." Curiously, there are many who are so filled with a sense of self pride that they can never publicly acknowledge that they were wrong.

Even more valuable than the ability to say "I'm sorry" is the capacity to make restitution for damage. Unfortunately, many, engulfed in their own sense of self-importance or self-righteousness, refuse to respond to guilt in such a direct manner.

A sense of guilt is most often like the beam from the lighthouse of our own conscience that attempts to guide us back into a safer and less dangerous route.

PART FIVE

The Unique Stresses
of the Holidays

CHAPTER 15

The Psychological Art
of Gift-Giving:

*M*ike V., age 40, bought his son, Kevin, age 2, a $200 set of electric trains. They were set up under the tree. Mike was furious when Kevin put the locomotive into his soapy bath.

Joe S., age 47, was delighted that his son passed his driving test on the first try. For Christmas, he bought him a brand new BMW.

Margaret V., age 61, gave her friend Janet, obese and trying to lose weight, a two-pound box of freshly baked cookies.

Dr. Philip S., age 38, just moved into town and joined the staff of the local hospital. Last year, during the holidays, he sent 20 colleagues he barely knew food baskets that cost more than $100 each.

Giving gifts is not as easy as it might seem. The right gift for the right person at the right time is not a simple task. Many years ago, an Englishwoman, Lady Pamela Glenconner, wrote, "Giving presents is a talent, to know what a person wants, to know when and how to get it, to give it lovingly and well. Unless a character possesses this talent, there is no moment more annihilating to lose than that in which a present is received and given..."

On the surface, giving a gift would appear to be a simple act of kindness and consideration. If you reflect back upon your own life and experiences, I'm sure you will remember incidences where you received a gift that made you uncomfortable or irritated. At other times, you would receive a gift; you would make appropriate thank you sounds and then would place the useless gift in the attic to wait for the next garage sale.

In order to improve your own gift-giving skills, let's explore some of the reasons that inappropriate gifts are chosen and given, often to the people whom we love. The inappropriate gift, rather than bringing pleasure and growth, can result in discomfort and pain.

1) The Gift That the Giver Would Want for Himself

Sometimes, unhappily, when we pick a gift, we buy a gift that we would secretly want. In doing so, we might completely ignore the appropriateness of the gift for the other person. When Mike V. bought his 2-year-old son a set of trains, he really was buying the trains for himself. Many a parent has been disappointed when they see their two year old is more fascinated by the carton that the gift came in rather than the gift itself. When Kevin's dad set up the new set of electric trains, he was bringing back distant echoes of his own childhood. Expecting his son to be delighted with the trains, he soon became disappointed at his son's normal short attention span. He became upset when his boy began to carry the locomotive around the house, and suddenly thought it was great fun to throw the new toy into his bathtub. His son, you see, at age two, really didn't understand the subtle differences between a train and a boat.

2) The Unconsciously Hostile Gift

Not so many years ago, there was a tribe of native Americans on the Pacific West Coast who had a peculiar custom called *Pot-Latch*. It was designed to embarrass and shame someone else. People in this tribe would ruin enemies by giving them gifts that would later have to be returned with interest. At a Pot-Latch, for example, Joe might give Sam a brand new boat, the latest in fishing gear and lots of food. The hidden purpose of this "giving orgy" was to humiliate the other person because they would no longer be able to afford to return to the next round of "can you top this?" While most people no longer throw Pot-Latches, it is not hard to find people who unconsciously express the hostility by giving gifts that will harm, rather than help, the recipient.

One patient of mine, for example, gave a large box of cookies to her friend who was morbidly obese and on a strict diet. Her friend, with some degree of thinly disguised anger, refused the gift. My patient, talking about this incident with me, was initially upset by her friend's refusal. As she spoke about her relationship with this friend, it became clear that she was, in many ways, involved in a longterm relationship that contained, mixed with admiration and good times, a considerable amount of jealousy, resentment and unexpressed anger. As she spoke more, it became obvious that her gift of cookies was really a gift of unconscious anger that was designed to sabotage her friend's most recent attempt to diet.

3) The Gift That Is Really a Bribe

I'm sure that many of you have had the experience of getting a gift that was inappropriate because it was either too large, too lavish or both. If, for example, you send your dentist's receptionist a large gift – under the guise of "holiday giving" – are you really giving her a gift or (be honest now!) are you giving *yourself* the gift of preferential access to the office the next time your tooth bothers you?

Up until recently, many major drug companies would give all kinds of elaborate gifts to physicians. These gifts have included expensive dinners, weekend vacations, and all manner of "toys" for the office and home. Although these gifts were given free, they were usually accompanied by considerable propaganda to the physician indicating why he should write a prescription for "drug X" instead of "drug Y" the next time he needed to treat a patient.

These elaborate gifts to the doctors, in the last analysis, were given not so much as a token of esteem to an admirable professional, but as a thinly disguised bribe.

4) The Gift That Shows How Powerful we Are

When Joe S.'s son, Bruce, passed his driving test the first time out, Joe S. was elated. He also was pleased that Bruce was doing well at school and seemed to be headed towards a prestigious college. In his state of bliss, he promised Bruce that he would buy him a car. His wife and friends suggested to Joe that Bruce's needs for his first car would best be served by getting him a solid, reliable, used "clunkmobile" so that he would be relatively safe when he got into his first traffic accident. Joe politely listened to all of the advice that was given to him and then went out and bought Bruce a brand new expensive sports car. His wife was annoyed but he justified his purchase by telling her that the car was rated very highly in safety tests and that it was important for Bruce to drive a reliable vehicle.

About three weeks after Bruce got his car, he had his first accident and a repair bill of close to $10,000. Joe was scared and then mad. "Why didn't you take better care of that beautiful car?" he kept yelling at Bruce. Bruce made the situation worse by yelling back: "I never needed such a car! I lost control on the wet leaves! I'll buy my own car next time!"

As Joe spoke about the whole event, it became clear what motivated him to buy Bruce the car. As a child, Joe grew up in an economically deprived home. His cousins, both on his mother's and father's side, were extremely prosperous. As a child, Joe had often felt left out and jealous. He still was in close contact with his cousins and their children who were all about the same age as Bruce. All of his cousins bought their children rather modest "first-car-mobile." Almost completely unaware of his true motivations, Joe bought the expensive sports car not so much for Bruce, but to show off to his cousins that he too was now prosperous and successful.

When someone gives someone else an expensive and often ostentatious gift, you might well ask "Hey! What's going on here?" Since there are so many issues involved in the exchange of gifts, what are some of the kinds of gifts that, in my experience, are the most valued and appreciated? Let's look at a few of them:

1) The Thoughtful Gift

It's easy to throw another tie under someone else's tree on Christmas day. It's harder, more challenging, and in the long run, much more fun for the giver, as well as the recipient, to give a gift that is thoughtful and individualized.

One woman that I know, for example, gave a dinner party in the spring. At the party, one of her best friends kept commenting about how much she enjoyed a particular onion relish that was served as an accompaniment to the roast. Making a mental note about her friend's enjoyment about this particular preparation, this woman contacted the producer and asked if they would ship the product. The manufacturer informed the caller that they did not ship the product, but gave her the name of a food market nearby that had the relish in stock. She purchased one dozen jars and presented them to her friend as a holiday gift. Much better than another scarf!!

A friend of mine is an avid golfer. When he plays in the summer, he usually carries a water bottle with him. He commented to a member of his regular foursome that he was having trouble closing the water bottle because the ridges on the cap were wearing down. At the holidays, it was the custom of this group to exchange small gifts. My friend was delighted when one of his golfing friends gave him a new, well-made water bottle. He commented several times "wasn't that thoughtful!" It was a much more meaningful gift than another dozen personalized golf balls.

2) The Creative Gift

After awhile, gift giving, all too often, becomes banal, automatic and quite stale. The bottle of wine, the box of candy, the selection of perfumed soaps – ho hum!! Yawn! Yawn! Yawn!

To freshen up your gift-giving, it can really help to tune into the creative part of your mind and come up with an idea and a gift that will really hit the mark. Curiously, many of the most creative gifts cost little in the way of money – but a lot in the way of time and effort. It is these gifts that are most often, in the long run, treasured and kept.

One woman, for example, wanted to give a special holiday gift to a friend who had just recovered from a nasty bout of chemotherapy for a cancer that fortunately was apparently in complete remission. This woman, realizing that her friend was an extremely gregarious person who had many friends, hit upon an unusual and creative idea. She, in collaboration with the woman's husband, wrote to approximately 100 of her friend's friends. She requested that each of them, if they could find the time, write a letter to her friend entitled, "Betty, this is what knowing you means to me."

She expected a response of perhaps 40 to 50 letters. To her surprise, she received more than 80 letters from friends far away and near. Some of these letters were four or five pages long and detailed old, almost forgotten anecdotes of adventures and events. Other letters were more brief, but in their brevity, were still able to convey a sense of friendship and love.

After all of the letters were received, the woman assembled them into a large album. Each page was carefully encased in plastic so the letters, and the envelopes with return addresses, would be carefully preserved. As could be imagined, her friend was delighted with the gift and in all sincerity, she called the giver and creator a few weeks later to tell her that, "It was the best gift that I could have received."

3) The Helpful Gift

All of us need help from time to time. Often, when we need help, we are too proud to ask. If someone who is close to us needs help, it often makes us anxious to see someone who was primarily seen as invincible and invulnerable in the need of assistance. Like a child who sees his/her father as a "Superman," we become unconsciously threatened by someone else's need for assistance.

I remember, for example, that when my daughter was about 3 years old, our house was hit by lightening on a Sunday afternoon. There was some smoke and sparks around the air-conditioner that was struck. In spite of the noise, the smoke and the sparks my daughter remained amazingly calm until I went to the phone to call the police and fire department. As I was finishing the call, my daughter asked, "Why are you calling the police, Daddy?" I replied calmly, "because Daddy might need some help." At that point, my daughter began to sob and grabbed my leg. She cried, "Why would my Daddy ever need help?" We all, on occasion, need some help.

One of the greatest gifts that we can give another person is to be aware and sensitive to the areas of their life that need some help. One elderly man, for example, had always been proud and strong. He took particular pride in his extensive flower garden filled with a vast collection of tulips and narcissus. Unhappily, as a result of severe arthritis, he could no longer spend comfortable time planting new selections. His nephew, aware and tuned in to his uncle's progressive disability, arrived one day in October with a bulb catalog from a leading seed company and announced, "Uncle Phil, I've decided what I'm getting for you this year. Here's the deal: You pick out 100 bulbs and I'll plant them for you wherever you want." Uncle Phil spent many happy hours picking out a new selection of hybrid tulips. They arrived in mid-November (he insisted on paying for them) and on one beautiful autumn Saturday, his nephew, true to his word, came to the house and planted the new bulbs under the direction of his uncle. "It's a gift to remember – and look forward to," he wrote to his nephew in a thank-you note. And you know what? It truly was!

4) The Gift of Teaching Someone Something New

If there is one outstanding characteristic of emotionally healthy, happy people, I would venture to say that it is their capacity and desire to learn and to grow. These people continue to learn and to master new skills throughout their lives.

It wasn't long ago that some psychologists believed that older people could not learn new skills as well as younger folks. Today, we know that the old adage "old dogs can't learn new tricks" is simply a bit of canine nonsense. Old dogs can learn new tricks, particularly if the new tricks are meaningful and important. As we get older, we tend to filter out irrelevant new knowledge, but we continue to learn important stuff.

If you think about the people you know, I'm sure you'll observe that those friends and relatives who tend to be happy and content with their lot are most often people who have learned a lot of skills that they enjoy improving and using these skills both with other people as well as when they are alone.

What a wonderful gift it is when you help someone learn a new skill that can then become part of their storehouse of abilities.

One father, a few years ago, decided to give his son a wonderful gift for the holiday. This man was a skilled electrical engineer and a good technician. When his son was 12 years old, he bought him a kit that contained all the material and instructions to make a color television. During many "shop sessions," this father taught his son how to read technical directions, how to solder and how to handle small electronic parts. You can just imagine the sense of pride this boy experienced when he plugged in the completed TV set and said, "Wow! It works!" The gift that was given to this boy will last long after his TV set is outmoded and scrapped. Indeed, the last time I had contact with this family, I learned that the young man was building his own stereo system.

5) The Gift of Self

Too often, in our thing-oriented culture, we equate giving with buying. This faulty equation can, at its best, lead to temporary happiness. Material gifts can be given by almost anyone (if they have a good credit line or lots of cash) and given to almost anyone (if they choose to receive the gift).

There are certain gifts that, in the long run, are more permanent and long-lasting. These are gifts that can be given only by you. It's a gift of self.

Several years ago, I worked with a young boy who had a severe behavior problem at home, in school and in the neighborhood. He was cranky and aggressive and got into fights with all of the other kids in the neighborhood.

His father was a successful professional man who was rarely at home. His mother was pursuing her studies for an advanced degree. The boy was cared for by a series of "nannies" who, after spending some time with this unpleasant boy, couldn't wait to leave and find another job. The parade of nannies went on and sometimes when the parents couldn't find a replacement, they would take the boy for a weekend to one of the plastic amusement parks.

Because of his difficult behavior, the parents began some counseling. They began to understand that the boy's frequent stomach aches were really "attention" aches and his acting out in school was a cry for help. Their understanding of his needs was soon implemented by a change in behavior. They began to spend much more time with their son. During this time, they tried to communicate, play and understand. Within a short period of time, his behavior began to improve at home, school and in the neighborhood.

This holiday season, could you consider giving a gift of time to someone you love? Some possibilities:

One evening a week for an uninterrupted family dinner.

A series of Saturday afternoon catches on the front lawn or at the skating rink.

A weekday evening with Monopoly, chess or checkers. No TV.

A mystery trip on the first Sunday afternoon of every month.

What fun it could be for you to present someone you love with a hand-written contract promising them something that they would love and only you could deliver.

As a psychologist, I have no objection to the giving of some well-chosen material gifts to those you love. Toys can be terrific and sweaters can be super – but the gift of self, that only you can give, will last for years and, if properly chosen, will never wear out.

Happy Giving!

CHAPTER 16

Beating the Holiday Blues - Before They Begin

DEAR DR. SUGARMAN: "Almost every year, without fail, my husband goes into a swoon of depression around the holidays – he gets lethargic, he's cynical (at least more than he usually is) and he drinks too much. Honestly, I'm tired of it! I see plenty of articles about 'Christmas Blues' which aren't of much help on Christmas. But do you suggest anything that can be done before the holidays to avert this? Any suggestions?"

Wow! This is a good question. Let's see if I can be of some help. While the holidays for some are filled with joy and happy family reunions, for all too many Americans the upcoming holidays bring sadness, disappointment and a global sense of physical and emotional malaise. Psychologists, psychiatrists and mental health clinics are all too familiar with the rush of emergency phone calls and requests for "extra" appointments.

In a now-famous study of life stressors that was done a few years ago, Christmas made the "Top 100" list. *Not exactly on top – it was behind getting divorced or fired – but, nevertheless, on the list*

Because the holidays are so stressful and unhappy for so many, you are quite correct in noting that magazines and newspapers sprout articles about dealing with holiday stress as frequently as empty lots fill up with Christmas trees for sale! Like an unsold Christmas tree on January 1, many of these articles are of little use *after the fact.* "Locking" the psychological "barn door" is not of much value after the "Holiday Blues Horse" has escaped.

As a practicing clinical psychologist, here are some things that you and your husband can try in order to prevent a rerun of your unhappy past holidays.

1) Cut Your Expectations Down to Size

Several years ago, I conducted a family therapy session during which the father said to his son, "You're an underachiever!" The boy thought a moment and then said, "I'm not an underachiever – maybe you're an overexpector." Like this boy's father, all too many of us are overexpectors when it comes to the holidays. An attitude of overexpectation dooms us to disappointment.

All of you, I am sure, have had the experience of friends raving about a particular movie. "It's the best movie ever made – you have to see it!" This statement almost always leads to "I didn't think it was so great." Had you discovered the same film on your own without so much hype, you could have enjoyed it much more. The day after Christmas, many people begin planning for their next Christmas. They buy half-price cards and ornaments as visions and hopes for next year begin to dance in their imagination. The dancing visions of next Christmas become more active in August when the holiday catalogues begin to arrive and it reaches a frenzy in November and December when the TV screen fills with images of happy joyous holiday celebrants.

If deep down you can really understand that, while holidays

can be pleasant and fun, they don't have to be spectacular and awesome, I suspect that you may be pleasantly surprised.

2) Learn to Say "NO"

As the year winds down, social activities and parties gear up. You are invited to cousin Sally's house and, after all, you *should* accept Uncle Mark's invitation to help with the tree. Then there's the office party, the neighbors cocktail party and... and and...! I think you know your list better than anyone!

In addition to demands on your time, the kids present you with Christmas lists for Santa that could bankrupt Ted Turner or Paul Getty. By not wanting to disappoint the kids, the friends, the neighbors and the family of cardinals that rely on your backyard birdfeeder, you often become overextended, unnecessarily stressed and irritable. Out of this unhappy brew, "holiday blues" begin to ferment.

Learn to say "NO." You can say it kindly and firmly – and in the long run everyone will be happier with the results. Your kids will *not* be traumatized by getting only 48 instead of 50 toys and your neighbor will understand that you just can't do another party this week. If you can prioritize those events and gifts that are truly important and forget the rest, I suspect you will have a much better holiday.

3) Keep It Simple

I remember seeing a family that spent hours ruminating and worrying about what kind of Christmas gift they should give to their 2-year-old daughter. After much thought, they bought an elaborate doll house that required hours to assemble. After many moments of frustration, the proud parents finally placed the batteries in the right holder and all of the rooms were illuminated.

They could hardly wait to present this thoughtful labor of love to their daughter. Christmas morning came and the child was suitably delighted and surprised – for about eight minutes. For the rest of the afternoon, the child seemed to be much more content playing with the cardboard carton in which the dollhouse arrived.

Like this child, so many of us really enjoy the simple joys of life. If you want to prevent holiday stress for you and your family, *keep it simple.* Simplicity in gifts, entertaining, dinners and cards all can be helpful. When you decorate your house, you need to remember that for every strand of lights that you use, almost inevitably, you will need extra time to replace a bulb. For every extra wreath that you put in the living room, there will be extra pine needles to sweep. For every extra gift you give in December, there will be an extra charge on your January credit card.

Remember: Simplicity and good taste are usually closely related.

4) Just Because You're Not the "Brady Bunch" Doesn't Mean You're the "Shady Bunch"

During the holidays, families reunite and come together from far and wide. They arrive with dreams, plans and lots of old resentments.

Once, during a family session, a teenage girl, disappointed that her brother had dropped out of college and upset about her father who was a recovering alcoholic, began the sessions by saying sadly, "Well, here we are – not the 'Brady Bunch' but the 'Shady Bunch.'"

When holidays bring large families together, old conflicts once again begin to boil and bubble. As surely as New Year's Day arrives a week after Christmas, when the family gathers, ghosts of old conflicts begin to surface. After the pumpkin pie, Uncle Chuck is sure to tell the story about how he was discouraged by

Uncle Bob from buying the first McDonald's franchise for a nominal sum. After the eggnog, Aunt Sara gets weepy and remembers cousin Phil who died of AIDS three years ago.

Listening to family interaction can make you feel that you're completely trapped by a strange and dysfunctional group! As an experienced psychologist, I can assure you that the notion of the completely "normal" family is simply a myth. This myth of the "normal" family can become dangerous and counterproductive if it leads to self-hate and feelings of having been cheated. Almost all families are a little "nuts" in their own ways. If you understand this, and don't lose your sense of perspective and humor, you'll be much more able to deal with the only family that you have, warts and all!

With a new and more tolerant attitude, you'll cut down on your stress and you might even begin to enjoy touching base with your imperfect family.

5) Take Care of That Wonderful Machine Called Your Body

Like a car that is poorly maintained, breaks down and strands us in the middle lane of the New Jersey Turnpike during rush hour, our bodies, if not maintained, can break down and foil us in the middle of Christmas dinner.

In order to prevent a physical or emotional breakdown, we need to spend a little extra care taking care of our health as we prepare for the holidays. It's hard to find time for a walk, a nap or a decent meal in the midst of shopping, wrapping, dining and calling but now, more than ever, it is necessary!

Preparations for the holiday can indeed be stressful, so you need to remember that it's even more important than usual to pay attention to your physical health. If a car, for example, is to be stressed by driving it extra hard over rough terrain, it's more important than ever to keep it well lubricated and maintained.

During your frantic preparations, take a little extra care of *you!* Don't neglect your exercise, take a long leisurely bath or take some "time-outs" and a night at home with no other distractions except the VCR. Get some extra rest. When we are too fatigued, we can't experience much happiness or joy.

6) Feel Your Feelings

One of the biggest muddles that people get themselves into happens when we deny what we are feeling – or worse – when we start telling ourselves that we "shouldn't" feel this way or that way. During the upcoming holiday season, in particular, there is enormous pressure on us to feel a particular way. From every loudspeaker in every shopping mall we hear "Joy, Happiest time of the year." After awhile, many people begin to feel that it's practically un-American not to feel happy at this time. Yet, if the truth be known, many of us may not be particularly happy because of events that are taking place in our lives or families. It is not pleasurable to feel unhappy but our unhappiness magnifies many times over when we tell ourselves things like "Everyone is so happy – what's the matter with me" or "Something must be terribly wrong with me – I just can't seem to get into the spirit of things. I must be a Grinch."

Remember, you're not responsible for your feelings, you're responsible for your actions. If we learn to accept a period of pre-holiday blues the feelings will soon pass. Like a wind blowing through leaves, feelings, if accepted, are almost always temporary.

If you are willing to accept a period of pre-holiday blues as normal and okay, you will certainly be on the road to a happier holiday.

CHAPTER 17

Making a New Year's Resolution Stick

It's January, the holiday ornaments are stashed away in the attic, the cookie jar only has a few crumbs left and, for many of you, those wonderful New Year resolutions are about as dead as the Christmas tree in front of your house awaiting "special" garbage pick-up!

During this time of year, almost invariably, a patient or two will say, "I don't know, Dr. Sugarman, I started off with such good intentions, but I can't stick with trying to break the habit of (fill in the blank). I guess I have no willpower!"

If you feel yourself in the uncomfortable spot of struggling to give up a bad habit, let us explore some of the things that psychologists have learned about habits in recent years.

Perhaps, the most important thing that you can know about habits is that they are *learned* behavior. In fact, habits are defined as being a "learned, fixed way of gratifying a need." The most fundamental thing to know about learning is probably that any behavior that *is rewarded* is likely to be learned. Most human behavior is not instinctive but is learned. Human beings are remarkably bright and malleable and so we can learn all kinds of healthy – or un-healthy – habits.

All human beings, for example, have a need to replenish our-selves by eating. Our bodies cry out for protein, and we feel this need as hunger. If you learned as a child that your appetite could be rewarded by beef, you are likely to grow up eating steak or hamburgers. If you learn that raw fish will help to quell hunger pangs, you grow up loving Sushi and so it is for lobster, pigs, stom-ach, snails, goat, cow's tongues and almost any other creature that walks, crawls or swims!! If a behavior is not rewarded in some ways, you quite simply will never learn it.

When you realize that your habits are learned, you can start or stop fooling yourself with statements such as, "I guess it's just in my genes," or "I can't change, I'm just built that way." Most im-portant of all is that it is important to remember that *whatever is learned can be unlearned!* So, if you truly want to *unlearn* some bad habits, here are some tips that are sure to help.

1) Be Specific in What You Want to Change

All too often, good New Year's resolutions go down the drain because they are too vague. A resolution such as "this year I want to live a healthier lifestyle" is doomed to fail. In order to change a habit, you need to pinpoint the behavior you want to change. By healthier lifestyle do you mean fewer calories, less overworking, less stress, more exercise, regular medical checkups? When you set out to change a bad habit, it helps a lot to specify *exactly* what behavior you want to change.

It also helps not to be too ambitious about changing every-thing at once. Remember, most of the habits that you want to change are bringing you some short-term pleasure, even though you know that the long-term consequences may not be too pleasant. To deprive yourself too much too soon is counterproductive.

For example, last year a patient of mine, with all good intentions, decided to take better care of his health. He made a resolution on January 1st that he would stop smoking and would limit his intake of fat and sugars. He also resolved to give up his nightly glass of wine. For two weeks, this man was uncomfortable and irritable. Needless to say, by January 20th, he was smoking, eating, and drinking more than ever. Saddest of all was the fact that he felt he was a failure and a weakling. How much better it would have been if he decided to just work on one of the habits that he needed to change.

2) Up the Ante

A few weeks ago, a woman said to me, "I would give anything if I could just lose 20 pounds. I've tried it so often but it never works. The best I ever did was about 12 pounds. I tell you Doc, I just can't do it."

After she told me her feelings of failure, I asked her to imagine a situation in which she was living in a kingdom that was ruled by a monarch who decided that if any subject in the kingdom did not lose 20 pounds within the year, all of their children would be beheaded in the public square. Knowing that she was extremely fond of her children, I asked her if she would be able to lose the 20 pounds, she replied immediately "What a silly question. Of course I would." Like this woman, many attempts to change a habit fail because the stakes seem to be too low. To ensure our success in changing a habit, it sometimes helps to raise the stakes.

One well-known psychologist has his Democratic patients write out a $500 dollar check to the Republican Party, and his Republican patients write a similar check made out to the Democratic Party. He holds the checks and promises to tear them up when the goal is achieved, if not, he mails them. To the best of my knowledge, no checks have yet been sent!

Try and find out what could "up the ante" for yourself. A $100 bet with your friend that you won't smoke until March 1st? Be creative!!

3) Locate the Buttons that Set the Habit Going

Like a CD that plays again and again when you push a button, habits are, for the most part, quite automatic. One of the most important tools that you can have when you try to chop a habit down to size is to find out where the buttons are that set off a habit.

Psychologists call these buttons "cues" and sometimes these cues are easy to spot. One man, for example, came to realize that he would automatically light a cigarette when the phone would ring or when he drank a cup of coffee. Sometimes, it's not as easy to "spot" the cues and a little detective work is often helpful. It is sometimes a good idea to keep a diary in which you enter the time, place, and actions that are taking place just before the old habit emerges.

A patient of mine, for example, was able to stay on her diet for long periods of time. Then, and seemingly without reason or cause, she would begin to binge. The puzzle persisted until she kept a diary of her eating behavior. When she did, she observed that her binges often took place following an unpleasant phone conversation with her unhappy mother. Armed with this knowledge, she learned not to call her mother from the phone in the kitchen. Even more valuable was the fact that eventually she learned to handle her feelings of anger in a better manner than to defeat her own goal of losing weight.

4) Don't Give Up – Take Up!

We human beings are funny creatures. Most of us prefer "addition" to "subtraction." If we approach changing a bad habit with the mind-set that we will be *giving* up something, we often make it much harder on ourselves than if we reframed our "mind-set" to think about *taking* up something. When we think about *giving* up something, we open up a whole mental file of loss, deprivation, and emptiness. When we think about *taking* up something, we open another more positive file that contains feelings of hope, expectation and fulfillment.

In my experience, the best thing that you can do when you try to change an unhappy or unhealthy habit is to formulate plans for substituting a healthier habit or behavior that can bring some pleasures. One man, for example, became concerned about the fact that he had gotten into the habit of having two or three drinks before dinner every night. He explained to me that he would arrive home from a long bus commute exhausted and drained. What started off as a nightly drink soon became two and then three. While the alcohol provided an immediate lift and a sense of pleasure, he soon noted that after supper, he felt even more fatigued and worse than when he arrived home. The next day he frequently felt depressed and vaguely nauseous.

In talking with this man about substitute activities, he devised a new plan. Now when he comes home, he changes his clothes and either walks or runs two to three miles. Afterwards, he takes a shower and has some tomato juice. He found that after a few weeks on this program, he got the same "lift" that he had previously gotten from alcohol – and guess what – an additional bonus, no hangovers!

5) Get Back on the Horse Right After You Fall Off!

Modern psychology has confirmed the folk wisdom that advises us to get right back on a horse after we have fallen off. By doing so, we don't let a fear incubate, grow and develop into a full-blown phobia. In giving up a bad habit, it is natural to sometimes "fall off the horse or slip from the wagon." All too often, these natural steps backwards are regarded by the person as a confirmation of the fact that they are helpless, hopeless and inadequate. They often perceive these temporary regressions as permanent failures. Studies have shown that when we give up a long – standing bad habit, occasional backward steps are to be expected. Research that has been down on people who eventually give up something forever indicates that most people quit smoking "permanently" about three times before the habit and the cigarettes are permanently extinguished.

All too often, a temporary "slip" kindles negative self-esteem and becomes the trigger to give up the new behavior entirely. One patient of mine, for example, battled his weight for many years, very unsuccessfully. There were times when he was in good control and he maintained his diet for months at a time. After such a long period he would occasionally, in an unguarded moment, accept the offer of a slice of cheese cake or an ice cream sundae. The next day, filled with anger at himself, he would tell himself that he "failed again" and "What's the use?"

A temporary lapse became a long-standing regression. He didn't lick his weight problem permanently until he enrolled in a weight reduction group where he learned to treat such setbacks as natural. Armed with this knowledge, he began to handle a brief setback in a different manner. Instead of "beating himself up," he went right back on the diet the next day. Remember, just because you slip, it doesn't mean you need to fall.

6) Reward Yourself

Psychologists know that there are both intrinsic and extrinsic rewards. Intrinsic rewards arise out of an activity itself while extrinsic rewards are sort of artificial dividends that are attached to doing or completing a specific task.

If, for example, you decide to take up the healthy habit of exercise, the intrinsic rewards of staying with this behavior will be a greater sense of well-being, more stamina and a better mood. An extrinsic reward would be a promise to treat yourself to a Broadway show after you have gone to the health club regularly for a few months.

In general it is more gratifying to receive intrinsic rewards.

Sometimes, in order to get started or to give ourselves a boost in our motivation, it is a good idea to attack an extrinsic reward to a behavior that we want to reinforce.

PART SIX

The Counseling & Therapy Option

CHAPTER 18

Psychological Counseling and Therapy:
How Helpful? How Often? How Much?

DEAR DR. SUGARMAN: "I have a friend who goes to a therapist once a week and he's been doing that for about five years. In the beginning, I thought it was a helpful and sensible thing for him but, in the last few years, it looks a little like a recreational activity. I think his insurance pays for part of it. What I'd like to know is how much counseling is appropriate for families or individuals? And is there such a thing as 'therapy dependency?'"

Yes and No!

This is a thoughtful question and there is no simple reply about your specific case. But, in order for you – or your friend – to answer the question correctly, let's explore this whole area of psychological counseling a bit so that both of you can become more knowledgeable and informed consumers of this helpful tool: Psychotherapy.

In all probability, counseling and psychotherapy existed from the time that cave men learned to talk and began to live in families and groups. People, as far as we can tell, have always had problems in living. I'm sure there were ancient people who were depressed, restless and in emotional conflict. There were probably cave-children who were excessively afraid of dinosaurs (phobic) and cave men who angered their wives by not making a fire in the cave (passive-aggressive). I'm confident that there were probably cave women who became overly upset and emotionally over-reactive to even slight problems (histrionic).

I'm equally sure that for these problems, as well as other problems in dealing with other people, the children or a difficult marriage, there were primitive forms of counseling and therapy. Since time eternal, people would seek the advice of a friend, a witch doctor, a healer or a religious shaman.

These ancient forms of counseling and psychotherapy are about as primitive as treating coronary artery disease with bleeding or treating cancer with mustard plasters applied to the affected organ.

Modern psychotherapeutic techniques began to evolve about a century ago, and since that time, enormous advances have been made in how to help people who are emotionally distressed.

The advances in counseling and helping people with emotional problems have not, however, been paralleled by public acceptance of psychotherapy or an awareness of what benefits can be accrued from helpful psychological interventions. Still, many people regard having an emotional problem – a depression or bouts of panic – as a sign of some sort of character flaw or a moral weakness. "Pull up your socks and stop feeling sorry for yourself" is often the attitude conveyed to the already suffering person.

One patient of mine, for example, suffering from severe obsessions and depression was berated by a co-worker when he related that he was in therapy. "Why do you need a crutch?" was the unsympathetic response. Another woman, who suffered from severe anxiety for years, had no hesitancy in visiting many physicians to see what help she could get in dealing with her headaches, her arthritis and her stomach distress – yet she "held out" seeking psychological help for a long time because she felt there was a stigma attached to psychotherapy. After a few sessions with a competent therapist, she began to experience considerable relief. "How silly it was of me," she verbalized after she felt better.

Other people, who may want to receive the benefits of counseling and therapy are bewildered by the multitude of professionals who offer counseling and the multiplicity of different approaches. If you're contemplating getting some psychological assistance or if you are already seeing a therapist and are wondering if you're getting maximum benefit from your sessions, here are some of the things about the some –what confusing field of therapy and counseling that you should know.

1) Who's Who?

The first thing you need to know is the fact that various trained professionals offer psychotherapy. Psychiatrists, psychologists, and psychiatric social workers represent the majority of professionals who offer psychological services to the public. The training in each of these professions is quite different.

Psychiatrists are physicians who, after medical school and receiving their M.D. degree, take a residency in psychiatry and with this training learn to deal with severe emotional illness. Psychologists, after receiving their Ph.D. in psychology, usually have an extended internship dealing with people who have behavioral problems or symptoms that they want to alter. Licensed social workers earn an M.S.W. degree in social work.

All of these professionals need to take stringent examinations in order to become licensed and to practice independently.

However, you should be aware that the title "psychotherapist" or "counselor" is not protected by licensing laws – and anyone –

regardless of training (or lack of) can offer up their services to the public. So, if you're looking for a therapist or counselor to assist you in dealing with some problems, make sure you find someone who is fully credentialed and licensed.

2) What's Right for You?

Even more confusing, perhaps, to the nonprofessional consumer of psychological services, is the fact that there are many different theoretical approaches to alleviating psychological problems and reducing emotional distress.

Let's explore a few of the major theoretical orientations that you are likely to encounter.

The *psychodynamic* approach, favored by many therapists, believes that most emotional conflict is rooted in early childhood experiences and trauma. Psychodynamic therapists believe that many of our behaviors and actions arise out of unconscious motivation and the goal of treatment is to help the patient become aware of what motivates them so that they can "move on" to healthier patterns of behavior. One man, for example, had many relationships with women that seemed to follow the same pattern. He would find himself very much in love for several weeks or months. After the relationship became closer and his partner began to move towards a longer term commitment, he began to find fault with her and soon the relationship would be over. In psychotherapy, he came to understand that his repeated self-destructive behavior was related to deep mistrust of women that resulted in observing, as a young child, his mother's abusive behavior towards his father. Helped by the insight and the support of his therapist, he finally became able to establish a gratifying long-term relationship with a woman who eventually became his wife.

The *behavioral* therapists, by contrast, believe that most behaviors we have are learned. They further believe that any behavior that is learned can be unlearned. In working with a person who has a marked phobia of bridges or elevators, the behavioral therapist will not be as interested in the origin of the fear – or its symbolic meaning – but rather will stress techniques that could help the patient *unlearn* the pattern of fear and avoidance. In doing this, the behavioral therapist might employ such techniques as teaching the patient relaxation or helping the person to have very gradual exposure to the feared situation.

Cognitive therapists stress that faulty thinking is at the root of much of our emotional distress and this therapy is aimed at changing unrealistic, often automatic, patterns of thinking. Depressed patients, for example, after making a human error such as forgetting an appointment, characteristically will say things to themselves such as, "Well, that's typical of me – I'm such a jerk – I've always been a loser and I guess that's the way I'm always going to be." By learning to identify and correct the errors in thinking, the patient often begins to think more realistically and, as a result, begins to feel better.

The *medically* oriented model of therapy tends to place emphasis on the biological changes that occur during periods of stress or anxiety. This model often views much of psychological distress as being the result of subtle "chemical imbalances" that may exist in the body and the suggested treatment is often medication that is designed to afford relief.

Some therapists may employ a variety of these techniques – but most have a favorite theoretical orientation which seems to work for them.

Interestingly enough, current research suggests that all of these approaches can be helpful at certain times and for certain people. It is, therefore, important for one – in choosing a therapist – to find someone whose ideas and methods of treatment seem to fit one's needs and orientation. Don't be afraid to ask a prospective therapist where he or she is theoretically coming from.

3) Male or Female – Young or Old

Therapists, like people, come in different ages, sexes and personalities. Since there are so many therapists around, you are lucky to have your choice of the person with whom you would like to work.

First of all, it is important that you find someone you can relate to with a certain degree of comfort.

You might prefer to work with someone who is older and perhaps has many years of experience. On the other hand, you might choose a therapist who has been more recently trained and is just beginning a career.

While studies have shown that the sex of the therapist has little to do with professional competence, your own preference should play a role here.

One adolescent girl, for example, made little progress with her male therapist. She found it hard to relate to him some of her feelings that occur when a girl becomes a woman, such as menstruation. When she transferred to a woman therapist, she felt herself able to speak more freely – and as she overcame her shyness, she became better able to verbalize her worries and concerns.

The personality of a therapist is always quite important. One therapist, for example, uses a considerable amount of humor in his sessions. Some of his patients are delighted as they begin to laugh at some of their maladjusted patterns of behavior. These patients feel helped. Other patients of this therapist view his humor as a "put-down." These patients feel they are being harmed.

In searching out a therapist, it is often best to get personal recommendations from ex-patients or other professionals who have had positive experiences with the person. There is nothing wrong in shopping around a bit before you settle into a counseling relationship.

4) You Have to Help the Helper

Here's a bad joke I'm sure many of you have heard.

Question: "How many psychologists does it take to change a light bulb?" *Answer:* "Only one – if it wants to be changed."

Like many jokes, this brief one contains some seeds of truth. All too many patients come to therapy with the expectation that the therapist will "do something" that will make them feel better. They are only too happy to assume a passive role in the hope that a wave of a magic wand will make them happy forever after – without any work or effort on their part. TOO BAD it doesn't work that way!!

Successful therapy depends on a good open collaborative relationship between two people. Most important, perhaps, is honesty. It's most vital – although not easy – for the patient to be completely honest with the therapist. Sometimes, a patient embarrassed or ashamed, does not give open disclosure and then wonders why progress is not being made. One patient of mine came to see me because of depression. After several months, he made little progress. Feeling that psychotherapy alone was not doing the job, I referred him to a psychiatrist who was an expert in prescribing antidepressant medication. After a rather prolonged period in which various medications were tried in addition to psychotherapy, he still did not improve. It wasn't until he revealed that he was smoking large amounts of marijuana every evening that the puzzle got solved. When initially questioned, early in our work, he denied using drugs except "once in a while – if I go to a big concert."

In addition to honesty, you can help the helper by doing some homework. If you're frightened by elevators, you might risk going up one floor in the elevator to see what happens.

If you're bored and come to the realization that your life is pretty stable and that it would be a good idea to take a course in college – sign up for it. Just don't talk about it! If you come to the realization that you are not assertive enough, try expressing your feelings. If you experiment with what you learn, I think you will be pleasantly surprised.

5) Stuck? Try a Consultation

Sometimes, therapy, goes along well for a period of time. Significant gains are made in many areas and, in general, you feel much better. There may be some areas, however, in which there seems to be no progress – in spite of all the effort and work that you have put into it.

Some "plateaus" are natural in learning any new behavior – but when a plateau continues too long – and you feel completely stuck – it may be time to talk to your therapist about your feelings and suggest that you have a consultation with another professional.

One mother, for example, made a lot of progress in dealing with her difficult teenage son who also had been seeing a therapist. He, in turn, was also making progress in his behavior. In spite of improvements, the mother was frustrated at her inability to break a pattern in which he didn't do his homework and she, in turn, would yell when she received progress reports from school. Recognizing the dilemma, her therapist suggested that she and her son have a consultation with an experienced family therapist. After three sessions of family therapy, the impasse was broken and mother and son continued to make progress in other areas.

6) You Decide How Much Therapy is Enough – and When it Should Begin or End

People come to therapy for different reasons and with very different goals. Sometimes a person's life, for the most part, is going well but a specific problem arises or a decision needs to be made that might require some choices. Often. this kind of problem can be solved by a few sessions of therapy in which the counselor helps the individual clarify the issues.

One man, for example, came to consult with me a couple of months ago. For the most part, he was well adjusted, his marriage and relationship with his children was solid and most of the time, he felt happy and content with his life. A problem arose, however, when he was offered an attractive job position in another city.

On one hand, he was very reluctant to move away from his friends and family and disrupt the lives of his wife and kids. On the other hand, he was attracted to the new job offer with its promise of future advancement and excitement. Caught in this conflict, he began to experience some symptoms of anxiety, sleeplessness and irritability.

After only four sessions of therapy that focused on helping him clarify his feelings and goals, he made his decision and his symptoms subsided. He had had enough therapy and did not need anymore. This situation is an example of brief, problem focused treatment.

For other people, therapy is a long term project. One woman, for example, had a disastrous childhood. She was abused, abandoned and made to feel worthless. She had been making slow but steady progress in therapy and after five years, she still continues to grow and is increasingly able to use her fine potential.

Five years ago, she was a high school dropout working in menial jobs and was engaged in a variety of destructive, promiscuous relationships. She now has an excellent job, has completed 60 college credits and has recently become engaged to a fine young man.

This patient's long-term therapy has served to function as a virtual reconstruction for a damaged personality and she has no intention of giving up a process which she regards as her "life-line and gyroscope." Now seen by her therapist twice a month, she continues to use her sessions productively.

Long-term therapy is often seen by those, who haven't experienced it, as an indulgence of the "worried well." For many people, it can make the difference between emotional illness and hospitalization or a life that becomes more tolerable and manageable.

Yes!, it would be great if we had an instantaneous cure of so many human conditions that distress us – but until we do, we have to be content with doing the best we can to ameliorate.

Does anyone mock or ridicule a diabetic who needs a daily injection of insulin to help them live a relatively normal life? Of course not! Why, then, should we ridicule a person with many deep-seated emotional problems for having a weekly session with a therapist who can help them stabilize their lives?

Recently, there has been tremendous pressure on patients in psychotherapy to limit the sessions to five or seven for the year. These pressures often come from HMOs who are interested in cutting costs and providing greater profit for their stockholders.

The thrust to limit mental health benefits comes in spite of the increasing evidence that patients who receive psychotherapy have less hospitalization and, therefore, cost less by reducing the need for expensive diagnostic procedures and tests. A recent study sponsored by *Consumer Reports* revealed that psychotherapy was an effective modality of treatment. Furthermore, this study demonstrated that for many people, the longer they remained in therapy, the better the results were.

Other studies have shown that, with some conditions, psychotherapy produces better and longer lasting effects than treatment with medication and produces fewer side effects.

How long should someone remain in counseling or therapy? My suggestion is that as long as sessions are productive and you are growing, it makes sense! If therapy becomes a rather stale habit, it is time to re-evaluate your goals and make some decisions that seem right for you. Remember, in the last analysis, you are the one who is in charge of your life!!

About Dr. Sugarman

Daniel Sugarman has been a practicing clinical psychologist for over 40 years. He received his Ph.D. in Clinical Psychology from Columbia University in 1957. He also holds an M.A. in Psychology from Columbia and a B.A. in psychology with honors from New York University. Since 1962 he has taught graduate and undergraduate courses in psychopathology and child development at William Paterson University in Wayne, New Jersey. A staff psychologist at St. Joseph's Hospital in Wayne, New Jersey, Dr. Sugarman is the author of five books on psychology and family therapy. His articles have appeared in such publications as *Reader's Digest, Woman's Day* and *Seventeen.* Dr. Sugarman and his wife, Barbara, live in Paramus, New Jersey, and they have three grown children. Dr. Sugarman can be reached via E-mail at dsugarmanph@aol.com.

Made in the USA
Monee, IL
06 August 2020

37741337R00103